Tolstoy

PLAYS

Tolstoy

PLAYS: VOLUME ONE, 1856–1886

Leo Tolstoy

Translated by Marvin Kantor with Tanya Tulchinsky

Introduction by Andrew Baruch Wachtel

Northwestern University Press

Evanston, Illinois

Northwestern University Press
Evanston, Illinois 60208-4210

Copyright © 1994 by Northwestern University
Press. All rights reserved.

Published 1994

Printed in the United States of America

**Library of Congress
Cataloging-in-Publication Data**

Tolstoy, Leo, graf, 1828–1910.
   [Plays. English]
   Tolstoy : plays / Leo Tolstoy ; translated by
   Marvin Kantor with Tanya Tulchinsky ;
   introduction by Andrew Baruch Wachtel.
        p. cm. — (European drama classics)
      Contents: t. 1. 1856–1886
      ISBN 0-8101-1109-8. — ISBN 0-8101-1110-1
   (pbk.)
      1. Tolstoy, Leo, graf, 1828–1910—Transla-
   tions into English. I. Kantor, Marvin. II. Tulchinsky, Tanya. III. Wachtel, Andrew Baruch. IV.
   Title. V. Series.
   PG3366.A19 1994
   891.72'3—dc20   94-22919
                                               CIP

The paper used in this publication meets the
minimum requirements of the American Nation-
al Standard for Information Sciences—Perma-
nence of Paper for Printed Library Materials,
ANSI Z39.48-1984.

Contents

Introduction

The image of Leo Tolstoy that comes to the mind of most readers is either the mature, confident, and self-sufficient author of *War and Peace* or *Anna Karenina*, or the older, iconoclastic, gray-bearded "sage of Yasnaya Polyana." In both cases, despite being surrounded by family and admirers, Tolstoy seems very much alone, sure of the importance both of his work and of himself, and unconcerned with whether he or it will be received as artistically, religiously, or politically correct. Naturally, these images are to a certain extent mythological, but they capture the self-image that Tolstoy wanted to project. What they fail to do, however, is to give us a picture of the younger Tolstoy, a writer who in the beginning stages of his career was very involved with the day-to-day literary and sociopolitical debates of Russia, and who strove in many of his early works to elbow his way into those debates, to find a place for himself in the hurly-burly of Russian literary life. It is this younger and less familiar Tolstoy who wrote most of the dramatic works presented in this volume (the first of a three-volume series that will contain all of Tolstoy's dramas), and it is difficult to understand these works without an appreciation of the complexities of Russian literary life in the mid-1850s.

Tolstoy had burst onto the Russian literary scene in 1852 with the publication of his pseudo-autobiographical novella *Childhood* in the leading literary journal of the day, *The Contemporary*. At the time the author was a twenty-four-year-old officer serving with the Russian army in the Caucasus. In the course of the next three years Tolstoy would remain in the army, publishing occasional stories based on military life in *The Contemporary*, including the powerful *Sebastopol Stories* of 1855–56. Toward the end of the Crimean War, however, Tolstoy decided to retire from the army and to move to Petersburg, the capital both of the Russian empire and of Russian intellectual life. He arrived in St. Petersburg at a most propitious moment; Tsar Nicholas I had died in early 1855, and his successor, Alexander II, was preparing to undertake the most extensive series of reforms since the age of Peter the Great. Russian society began to take up the "accursed questions" that had mostly been ignored during the authoritarian reign of Nicholas. The most important of these questions was serfdom (which would be abolished by decree in 1861), but others high on the list included the "woman question," as well as legal, military, and educational reform. The writers who had grouped themselves around *The Contemporary*, including the poet Nikolay Nekrasov (the journal's editor-in-chief), the critics Nikolay Chernyshevsky and Nikolay Dobrolyubov, and the novelist Ivan Turgenev, were in the midst of the struggle to liberalize Russia. Their political positions ranged from the radical (Dobrolyubov and Chernyshevsky) to the liberal (Turgenev), but they all would have agreed with the assumption that literature should play a leading role in the social and political life of the country. Although most of Tolstoy's early work was autobiographical in character, he had published it all in *The Contemporary* and this was naturally the group toward which the young Tolstoy gravitated in Petersburg, interacting at first in friendly fashion and later acrimoniously. Indeed, it was precisely as a result of these interactions that Tolstoy came to realize just how alienated he was from all of the existing camps of Russian thought, and this realization eventually led him to the splendid isolation of Yasnaya Polyana. It was in this brief period of interaction with the "most progressive" Russian minds that Tolstoy began sketching out his early dramas, which grew out of his increasingly negative attitudes to the ideas that surrounded him in St. Petersburg.

Tolstoy's first dramatic fragments date from 1856, and include *A Family of Gentlefolk*, *A Practical Man*, *An Uncle's Blessing*, and *Free Love*. The former pair are clearly a working out of one and the same idea under two titles, and a concern with this idea was sparked by Tolstoy's rocky relations with the slightly older and better-established Turgenev. On a personal level, the two had a love/hate relationship from the beginning of their acquaintance in 1856.[1] Turgenev possessed a classic liberal's tendency to tolerance which could easily shade into moral weakness and disengagement. Tolstoy, on the other hand, generally took uncompromising stands, and could not abide Turgenev's more tolerant nature. This difference is clearly apparent in the attitudes the two men took toward the gentry class to which they both belonged. The standard plot of a Turgenev work from about this time as well as later (including the novel *Rudin* [1856], and his most famous play, the comedy *A Month in the Country* [1850]), revolves around a gentry family living on its country estate. An outsider appears in their midst, and, through the interactions of this outsider with the family, we come to see the moral weaknesses of both the family and the outsider. As a rule, these weaknesses are treated gently, with a great deal of sympathy, and while we may laugh at some of the characters, they are more to be pitied than castigated.

The family Tolstoy describes in his earliest dramatic sketches (variously called the Zatsepins or the Kolomins), however, is treated with far more satirical caricature and far less indulgence. The members of the older generation clearly hate each other and are completely incapable of adjusting to a changing world. The younger generation, which consists of two brothers of opposing personalities, is either completely callous (the older brother) or completely helpless (the younger). The latter, whom Tolstoy in his notes characterized as "a Hamlet of our time,"[2] is a caricature of one of Turgenev's favorite character types (presented most notably in his story "A Hamlet of the Shchigrov District"), but again whereas Turgenev treats this type with a certain degree of sympathy, in Tolstoy's drama the younger brother is simply ineffectual. At the same time, it is difficult to tell from these sketches exactly what Tolstoy had in mind other than a general desire to attack Turgenev's overly poeticized view of the collapse of the gentry class, because at this point in his career he was unsure of how to proceed with a dramatic work. While we can see here a satirist's sharp eye and tongue, it is hard to discern much talent for dramatic writing.

The second set of sketches (*An Uncle's Blessing* and *Free Love*) also forms a clear pair, but the question to which Tolstoy turns his satiric eye this time is not the collapse of a gentry family but that of woman's liberation. Of course, the immediate source for Tolstoy's viciously negative portrayal of a "liberated woman" as a debauched harlot were the novels and the persona of the then immensely popular George Sand. Indeed, it is known that Tolstoy's public attacks on George Sand and her heroines caused a mini-scandal in the group around *The Contemporary*.[3] It is interesting, however, that whereas in his earlier dramatic sketches Tolstoy was entering onto well-charted territory, here he seems to have anticipated the debates that were soon to arise around the issue of woman's liberation in Russia. According to the leading historian on this subject: "The first serious discussion of the 'woman question' in Russia was undertaken by a man, the poet and radical publicist M. L. Mikhailov...between 1859 and his death in 1865."[4] Thus, it turns out that Tolstoy was already writing an anti-woman's liberation work before any pro-woman's liberation works had appeared in Russian literature. As was the case with his earlier sketches, however, it is obvious that although the young Tolstoy was able to produce a satiric sketch, he was unsure of how to create a play around this topic. Nevertheless, these early negative portraits of Sandian feminists would serve him in good stead when he returned to writing drama some seven years later.

Having been unable to finish his dramatic sketches of 1856, Tolstoy was not to try his hand at dramatic form again until 1863. Clearly he had not forgotten the themes of his earlier efforts, however, and when he returned to drama, he did so not by starting from scratch, but by knitting together the themes of his earlier sketches into a complete play. That he was able to do so does not so much attest to his greater artistic maturity as it does to the appearance of a new set of literary works against which Tolstoy could write. *An Infected Family* is, in fact, Tolstoy's contribution to perhaps the most famous and acrimonious debate in the history of Russian literature: the polemic spawned by the appearance of Turgenev's greatest novel, *Fathers and Children*, in 1862.

Fathers and Children explores the relationship of the generation of Russian liberals, the so-called men of the forties (Turgenev's own generation), with that of the radical "men of the sixties" (the generation of Chernyshevsky, Dobrolyubov, and their followers). Turgenev accomplishes this task symbolically, primarily through a presentation of the interactions between two generations of the Kirsanov family—on the one hand the young student Arkady Kirsanov, and on the other, his father and uncle. The most controversial character in the book, however, is young Kirsanov's friend Bazarov, who was radicalized in the course of his studies in Moscow. The latter belongs not to the aristocratic class, but is rather the son of a poor country doctor. He is by far the most powerful, intelligent, and compelling figure in the novel, and although he dies futilely in the end, it is nevertheless clear that despite pointing out a number of shortcomings in Bazarov's character, Turgenev had a great deal of sympathy for him. In the increasingly radicalized world of Russian politics of the early 1860s, however, Turgenev's attempt at a fair-minded portrayal of the new generation was unacceptable both to conservatives and particularly to the radicals.

Two famous replies to Turgenev's novel appeared almost immediately. The first was a critical article by Maksim Antonovich in *The Contemporary* (with which, by this time, Turgenev had broken). Antonovich attacked Turgenev's work, claiming that it was a didactic novel and a bad one at that, and insisting that the whole thing was merely a thinly disguised attempt to slander the entire new generation. An even more important rejoinder, however, was the utopian novel written by Chernyshevsky entitled *What Is To Be Done?* and published through an almost unbelievable oversight of the censorship in 1863, despite the fact that its author was in prison under a charge of sedition at the time. *What Is To Be Done?*, subtitled "From Stories about the New People," was a thoroughgoing attempt to depict the coming socialist utopia. Through his description of the feminist heroine Vera Pavlovna, the ultimate revolutionary Rakhmetov, and Vera Pavlovna's perfectly idealistic husbands, the doctors Lopukhov and Kirsanov, Chernyshevsky painted a picture of what could be accomplished through the application of "rational egoism" (the utilitarian belief that everyone acts in his or her own best interests and that, somehow, if everyone is brought to understand what his or her own best interests really are, then everyone acting individually will create utopia on earth).

The novels of Turgenev and Chernyshevsky ushered in a gigantic literary free-for-all. Practically all the major and many of the minor Russian writers got into the act and produced, over the next few years, a whole series of "nihilist" (the word had been brought into public discourse by Turgenev in *Fathers and Children*) and "anti-nihilist" novels.[5] Of these, by far the most famous today is Dostoevsky's *Notes from Underground*, although its real connection with this polemic was not recognized until the twentieth century.[6] While fictional quality as well as quantity were mostly on the side of the anti-nihilists, Chernyshevsky's novel went on to become perhaps the most widely read and influential work in Russia in the second half of the nineteenth century. As described by an anti-Chernyshevskyite professor:

> *What Is To Be Done?* is not only an encyclopedia, a reference book, but a codex for the practical application of the new word. ... In the guise of a novel (an awkward novel, an extremely coarse one), a complete guide to the remaking of social relations is offered: most important to

the remaking of the relations between men and women. ... In my sixteen years at the university I never did meet a student who had not read the famous novel while he was still in school. A fifth- or sixth-grade girl was considered a fool if she was unacquainted with the adventures of Vera Pavlovna. In this respect, the works, for example, of Turgenev or Goncharov—not to mention Gogol or Pushkin—are far behind the novel *What Is To Be Done?*[7]

To all but scholars of Russian literature, Tolstoy's relationship to this burgeoning polemic is not well known. True, Tolstoy never did like Chernyshevsky very much, as is attested to by one famous letter to Nekrasov in which, among other things, he called Chernyshevsky "that bedbug-smelling gentleman."[8] Furthermore, he makes an obvious crack at the questionable logic of Nikolay Levin's Chernyshevsky-inspired friend (who wants to set up a locksmith's cooperative in a village that has no need for locks) in *Anna Karenina*. But Tolstoy's most extended reply to this literary and social hullabaloo is contained in his play *The Infected Family*. This play clearly reworks the same themes that had concerned Tolstoy in his earlier dramatic sketches, but now, in the context of the novels of Turgenev and Chernyshevsky, Tolstoy was able to complete an entire drama.

As in Turgenev's novel, *The Infected Family* revolves around a lack of understanding between parents and children, in this case primarily the landowner Ivan Pribyshev, his daughter Lyubov, and his son Pyotr. Furthermore, as is again typical of Turgenev's plots, the rift between parents and children is brought to the surface through the appearance of "outsiders"; but these outsiders, the carriers of the "infection," are for the most part caricatures not of Turgenev's characters but of Chernyshevsky's. Anatoly Dmitrievich Venerovsky, the liberal whose passionate desire to "develop" his future bride conceals more selfish motives, is a parodic version of Chernyshevsky's Lopukhov (who in *What Is To Be Done?* "rescues" the heroine Vera Pavlovna from the clutches of her oppressive family). Pribyshev's niece, Katerina Matveyevna, is clearly attempting to model herself on Vera Pavlovna, as is revealed both by her passionate desire to join a commune and her sexual relations with both male characters. The student, Aleksey Pavlovich Tverdynskoy, is simply a hypocrite who mouths radical slogans about the equality of men and women but is not above making lewd advances to Katerina Matveyevna when the opportunity arises.

As opposed to Chernyshevsky's positive characterizations and Turgenev's tendency to portray everyone sympathetically, revealing both their strengths and weaknesses, however, Tolstoy presents only the negative qualities of his characters. Even the characters who eventually turn out to possess a grain of moral sense, including Ivan Mikhailovich Pribyshev and his daughter Lyubov Ivanovna, spend most of the play foolishly deluding themselves until the disastrous denouement mobilizes their immune system to fight off the Chernyshevskian infection. The only character who shows good sense throughout is Marya Isaevna, whose peasant outlook has presumably inoculated her against the urban foolishness which threatens to turn the Pribyshevs' life upside down.

Still and all, despite the fact that Tolstoy was able to finish this play, it must be considered an artistic failure. While it contains a number of amusingly nasty scenes, it neither grips the reader dramatically nor does it break new ground in terms of the social and intellectual debates of the time. Nevertheless, in 1864 the subject was quite topical and Tolstoy went to some trouble to have his play produced. Getting permission to stage a dramatic work in Russia in the mid-nineteenth century was no easy matter; a play had to be approved by both the regular censor and a theatrical censor as well as by a theater board. Although one of the directors of Moscow's Maly Theater was interested in Tolstoy's work, it soon became apparent that it could not possibly be performed during the 1864 season. Realizing this (and perhaps hearing second-hand the extremely negative reaction to his play of the great Russian playwright Alexander Ostrovsky),[9] Tolstoy lost interest in *The Infected Family*, returned to Yasnaya Polyana, and took up the far more fruitful project of writing *War and Peace*. Indeed, so thoroughly did Tolstoy forget about his play that he never even asked for the manuscript back. This final draft was eventually lost, and the text translated here was reconstructed long after the writer's death on the basis of drafts that remained in Tolstoy's archive.

The final dramatic fragment of Tolstoy's relating to the conflict of the generations is *The Nihilist*, which dates from 1866. These brief scenes are all that remain of a drama that the Tolstoy family seems to have written more or less by committee in order to put something on in their own home. As usual, the play was to revolve around a gentry family whose house was to be visited by outsiders including a student who believes in the "new ideas." This version of the old Turgenevian chestnut, however, seems to have been planned more as a farce than as a nasty satire. Even in the scenes that have survived, it is clear that we have a case of mistaken identity (the misinterpretation of an action, that is), rather than a serious attempt by the student to behave like a scoundrel. For a change, everything seems to end happily, although as usual it appears that Tolstoy does not really know what he wants to do with this chunk of theatrical material.

Ultimately, like all his other dramatic fragments on this topic, *The Nihilist* reveals that at this stage of his career, Tolstoy was either unable to pull together a successful dramatic work or insufficiently interested to do so. After *The Nihilist* Tolstoy was not to return to the dramatic form for almost two decades. By 1886, the year in which he wrote and published *The First Moonshiner*, sketched out his *Dramatization of the Legend about Aggeus,* and began his first successful full-length play, *The Realm of Darkness,* Tolstoy was a very different writer from the young man who had written dramatic sketches devoted to the conflict of the generations. Not only had he completed and published his two masterpieces *War and Peace* and *Anna Karenina,* but he had undergone a spiritual crisis and conversion and had, for the most part, rejected his previous literary style. In the mid-1880s Tolstoy was writing a whole series of fables, parables, legends, and fairy tales meant to be universally comprehensible and designed to be read by the Russian lower classes.[10] These works were to have a clear moral message, yet they were also to be artistically convincing. Among the more famous short fictional works that Tolstoy produced in this vein are the stories "What Do Men Live By" and "How Much Land Does a Man Need?" In addition, it was at this time that Tolstoy produced his own version of the gospels, which rejected all of the supernatural elements of the canonic gospels, while retaining what, in Tolstoy's opinion, was central to Jesus' teaching.

The legend of Aggeus exists in both Eastern and Western folk variants, and probably came to Russia through Poland. Tolstoy was clearly attracted to the subject because of its moral theme: the repentence of a rich man. The play itself is modeled after the popular entertainments of the

Russian "balagany" or fairground spectacles, many of which tended to mix theatrical affects with a moral message meant for the mostly illiterate spectators. Tolstoy never attempted to publish this play. It was found in his notebooks and published only in 1926. *The First Moonshiner,* on the other hand, was written in response to a letter from an actor named P. A. Denisenko who requested permission to rewrite some of Tolstoy's short moralistic stories for the stage. Tolstoy was taken by this idea and himself revised his earlier story "How the Demon Earned His Bread." The play was completed in early 1886 and it was submitted to the censorship soon afterward. By the summer of 1886 it was being performed by a number of "peoples' theater" companies on "balagan" stages in the capital.

As is the case with the best of Tolstoy's short stories of this type, *The First Moonshiner* is quite charming. The characters, both demonic and human, are well drawn, although naturally exaggerated for comic affect, and he puts peasant language to good use. The scenes in hell are particularly amusing, and, on the whole, this play gives the lie to the opinion that Tolstoy's moralizing works are literary failures. Still, from the point of view of "high" literature, neither *The Legend of Aggeus* nor *The First Moonshiner* can be seen as important works. However, in the same year that these plays were written, Tolstoy began *The Realm of Darkness,* a play which combines the theme of sin and repentence with the use of peasant language onstage in a shatteringly powerful drama. After a theatrical apprenticeship that stretched from his first dramatic sketches of 1856 to the moralizing plays of 1886, Tolstoy was ready by late 1886 to complete his first major work for the stage.[11]

Andrew Baruch Wachtel
Evanston, Ill.

A Family of Gentlefolk

A Comedy in Three Acts

Prince [Osip Ivanych] Zatsepin
retired Colonel in the Guards, 50
Princess
his wife, 40
Prince Anatoly [Osipych]
*his eldest son, a Lieutenant in
the Guards, 27*
Prince Valeryan
[Volinka] [Osipych]
*his youngest son, 20, has not
completed his course of studies
at the university, and is not in
the service*
Young Princess [Mashenka]
Prince Anatoly's wife, 19
Volodya
[Vladimir Petrovich, Volodka]
*steward, the old Prince's
former serf, 40*
Natalya [Dmitrevna]
his wife, 35
Pashenka
Natalya's sister, 22

Ivan Ilich
*illegitimate son of the father
of the old Prince, retired junior
officer in the cavalry, 43; has
already lived in the Prince's
home for fifteen years*
Overseer
Egorka
the old Prince's servant, 56
Eremey
Volodya's servant
Hyppolite
Prince Anatoly's servant
Sashka [Sasha]
the Princess's servant
Lyolya Zhitova
the Prince's neighbor
The Zhitovs' foreman's wife

*The action takes place in Prince
Zatsepin's village.*

Throughout the volume, additional information has been provided in brackets.

ACT I

A room next to the study, sofas all around; a round table in the center is set with a samovar, a silver coffee pot, cups, cream, biscuits, bread, and butter. At the table sit the old PRINCESS, *pouring tea, and* IVAN ILICH, *timidly buttering bread.* SASHKA *stands by the door, relaxed.*

PRINCESS. So, Ivan Ilich, you still haven't seen my husband today? I'm afraid he had a bad night's sleep again. Yesterday those peasant women, the ones that came to complain, aggravated him—oh, these people! And they say—village life is peaceful—he doesn't have a day go by without some sort of problems and troubles. Why haven't you looked in on him, Ivan Ilich, why haven't you looked in on my husband?

IVAN ILICH. I've been up to his door already, Princess. I'm reliable as a good watch—as the Prince is wont to say: I'm on my feet at seven o'clock; I walk to the mill and back by eight, and at eight I'm on my way to the Prince for tea. Natalya Dmitrevna was there, the master sent for her to clean out the comb, so I asked: may I enter? No, she says, the Prince'll come out right away himself, he's dressing already. How rich these biscuits are today, ma'am, Zakhar makes them good—in fact really great.

PRINCESS. Well, and have you seen my son Volinka?

IVAN ILICH. I have, Princess. He's in the garden. He's lying with a book near the greenhouse. I happened by, he didn't notice me. He reads so seriously. What an angel, that Valeryan Osipych of yours, that's what they all say, the servants and the neighbors. That's really so, he's been with us for three months and you never hear him, as if he weren't around. And how clever, too!

PRINCESS (*inattentively*). Yes ... Sasha, my friend, run down to the garden and tell Valeryan Osipych that his mama told you to say that, he should, she says, come to the house and get dressed for tea, otherwise Papa'll be there and'll be angry again that you're not there, you hear.

SASHKA. Yes, madam. (*Exits.*)

IVAN ILICH (*shouts after him*). Take care not to get into the raspberries. If Akim catches you, he'll let you have it. (*Silence.*)

PRINCESS. Do you want more tea or coffee?

IVAN ILICH. Some coffee now, please.

PRINCESS. Where did you go yesterday?

IVAN ILICH. To your neighbors, Princess, the Zaitsovs. They're nice people, they've also got a billiard table. The things we talked about there, Princess...

PRINCESS. What things?

IVAN ILICH. About Prince Osip Ivanych.

PRINCESS. My husband was saying these neighbors are not, he thinks, really nice people.

IVAN ILICH. No, Princess, they are worthy people. They said that they certainly want to ask the Prince to be Marshal. For next year.

PRINCESS. What nonsense—with his health! As it is there are too many disturbances, what's more, while our means are sufficient for us and for our children, we can't be giving banquets. And why should we. As far as I'm concerned, my husband has served enough.

IVAN ILICH. But they say the Prince, all the same, whatever his means, is the foremost person in the district in intelligence...

PRINCESS. I should say so.

IVAN ILICH. ...and in education, and in his connections, and in all respects. And about you they say, for a reception there's no such lady, like you and the governor's wife.

PRINCESS. Really, Ivan Ilich, you're a terrible gossip.

IVAN ILICH. They also talked about Vladimir Petrovich, Princess.

PRINCESS. About Volodya? What business of theirs is Volodya?

IVAN ILICH. There was one fellow there, the surveyor Bersov, who had business with him, he's very dissatisfied with him. And he said that if they elect the Prince, it won't be the Prince—I'm just repeating his words—but Volodka and Natalya who'll be Marshals.

PRINCESS (*sternly*). I told you once and I'm repeating it once and for all, don't you dare speak to me, either about Volodya or about Natalya. I know Volodya's relations with my husband, and I don't want to know how they are misconstrued.

IVAN ILICH. But, you know, I didn't say it, I just...

PRINCESS. All the same, you must not repeat it in my presence.

IVAN ILICH (*embarrassed*). I beg your pardon, Princess, believe me...

PRINCESS. Well now, hadn't you better go to the Prince and inquire about his health? And if he doesn't want to come out here, what should be sent to him there? Ask him also if he wants some fresh bread.

IVAN ILICH (*rises; at the door he meets the* PRINCE). Ah, the Princess was just sending me to inquire about your health, Your Excellency.

PRINCE (*annoyedly swinging his hands about* IVAN ILICH's *face*). Well, how's my health? Of course, lousy, and even worse because I don't have a moment's peace without some messenger running in. "Is your health alright, how did you sleep?" Ah, it's sickening. (*Goes to the table with the tea service. Enter* SASHKA.)

PRINCESS (*motions to him; he goes over to her*). Well, what is it?

SASHKA. He said he's coming.

PRINCESS. So has he gotten up? Is he on his way?

SASHKA. No, he's still lying there. I told him again to please come, he got mad. "Don't bother me," he said, and began reading again.

PRINCESS. Well, run over one more time. (*Rises and aside.*) Again this will irritate him, oh, my God! (*To her husband: kissing hand in hand.*) Good morning, my dear, did you sleep well?

PRINCE (*ironically*). Wonderfully...

PRINCESS (*sits down at the table*). Would you like some coffee, dear?

PRINCE. Yes. Only please not sweet as usual, like syrup. Isn't Valeryan here?

PRINCESS. He's in the garden, reading. He'll be here momentarily, dear. How about some biscuits? (*Hands them to him.*)

PRINCE. He's reading *Bestimmung des Menschen.*[1] A philosopher, to be sure! And that his father once told him he wants to see him at breakfast, that's nothing. But he's a master at talking. With the priest about philosophy, and impressing simpleton landowners with his words, that's the only thing he's good at.

PRINCESS. But he's preparing, you know, for an exam, dear, and sometimes reads too much, gets carried away.

PRINCE. Ah, I've had it up to here with that exam, my good wife. The same will come of that there exam as did from his farming, from his painting, from his service: he'll begin and drop it, that much I can tell you. I know him. If he wanted to study, he would've studied while he was at the university, he wouldn't have failed his exams and shamed me before all the professors, before the sponsor to whom I wrote about him. He's a loafer and nothing more.

PRINCESS. Ah dear, he's trying now.

PRINCE. He can't be trying anything, because he's an entirely trivial person, not capable of anything. (*Addressing* IVAN ILICH.) And all for what? Because the good wife and aunty, her sister in Moscow, got carried away with him and assured everyone, and him, too, that he's a genius and smart; now just look, he's simply a first-class dummy. That's what I've seen him be in these three months. (*Addressing his wife again.*) Dense as a cork, like that Sashka, dense and lazy, and a good-for-nothing, and that's all.

PRINCESS. Ah, why do you say this, my dear?

PRINCE. I'm not to blame for this, but you, madam, have a guilty conscience. The dummy is twenty years old, I took him to the governor, he didn't even know how to walk into the room, he couldn't say two words. The governor is a friend of mine and an old pal.

IVAN ILICH. Of course, Your Excellency, everyone knows, how he respects you.

PRINCE. Well he was just a boy, a cornet, when I was a lieutenant in the Guards, and he would come running to me as much as three times a day—that's what kind of relationship we have, but I'm embarrassed, ashamed before him for my son. You see he has forgotten how to speak French, he can no longer carry on *une conversation suivie* in French. He's some sort of clergy brat,[2] not a Prince Zatsepin.

PRINCESS. But he's still so young, my dear.

PRINCE. Young? I really like that; why for goodness' sake, my good wife, at his age I was already the Prince's adjutant, and all of Petersburg already knew me, but he's just preparing to take his qualifying exam. Young?

VOLODYA (*enters with a letter and bows to the* PRINCESS). Good morning, Your Excellency. They've come from town, and there's a letter for you, sir, I think from Prince Anatoly Osipych.

PRINCE. Give it here. Do you want some tea?

VOLODYA. Thank you, sir, I had some at home.

PRINCE (*unsealing the letter*). Pour him some tea. (*Reads.*) Ah! well fine, I'm very happy.

PRINCESS. What is it, my dear?

PRINCE. Prince Anatoly will be here any time now, he's taken leave for three months and is coming here with his wife. Only they'll not have much room. Eh? Volodya? What do you think? Where should we put them?

VOLODYA (*taking the cup*). Well, the coach house can be prepared.

PRINCE. Yes, yes, in the coach house. See to it that it's cleaned up, waxed, you know, so that it's neat. He'll be here today or tomorrow, he writes that he's leaving on the eighteenth: eighteenth, nineteenth, twentieth, twenty-first, yes, he could be here today; be so good, Volodya.

VOLODYA. Yes, sir; only wouldn't it be better to give them my coach house? And we would move.

PRINCESS. Quite right, dear, it's much better there, besides dear Mashenka, they say, is often ailing, and it's warmer there at night.

IVAN ILICH. It's clean, nice, and there's an entrance directly into the garden.

VOLODYA. But then again, it'll be fine in the other one, too.

PRINCE. Well, so? Huh? Volodya?

VOLODYA. As you wish.

PRINCE. No, let it be like I said at first.

PRINCESS. What does he write, my dear? Are they all healthy?

PRINCE. He writes that the general gave him leave, that, thank God, his service is going well, he's expecting a promotion. Now this one doesn't talk much about *Bestimmung des Menschen*, but is a doer. He's already an adjutant, a lieutenant in the Guards, in the best society, a good-looking fellow. Huh Volodya? Do you remember him? Huh?

VOLODYA. Of course.

PRINCE. I'm very happy, very happy, and she must be sweet. I knew and liked her father, he's a senator now, that's all good. I'm very happy, very happy. Huh, Volodya? She's got a nice fortune. They receive guests. Nice. Nice? Huh, Volodya?

SASHKA (*enters and whispers to the* PRINCESS). He said that he'll come right away, just a little more to read.

PRINCESS. Ah, my God! What a person! Give me the parasol, Sasha. Won't you have more to drink? I'm going to the garden, my dear.

PRINCE. Ivan Ilich, what, did you fall asleep?

IVAN ILICH. Not at all, sir—I'm happy, sir, that the young Prince'll be coming.

PRINCE. Go and rack the balls, I'll be in the billiard room right away, we'll play.

Scenario of the Comedy A Family of Gentlefolk

ACT I

Scene 1
At tea the Princess and Ivan Ilich speak about the Prince, {about marrying off Valeryan}* and about Anatoly. Ivan Ilich tattles on Natalya and Pashenka, and expects that things will go badly for them.

Scene 2
The Prince enters, scolds his son for not being there, and says that no one will marry him.

Scene 3
Volodya enters {with a letter from Anatoly}. The Prince praises his son enthusiastically and is concerned about where to put him; {afterwards he speaks about Valeryan, and Volodya sees him as an utter fool and tells about him and his relations with the peasants}.

Scene 4
The Princess leaves. Volodya {bored and suspicious} asks for orders. Ivan Ilich gossips about the Princess.

Scene 5
Volodya pokes fun at Ivan Ilych, they leave to rack the balls. The Prince {is alone, angry with his wife, son, the peasant, and even Volodya} is weary, only Volodya and Natalya are good people.

Scene 6
Enter Pashenka. The Prince touches her. She says that he has a wife and Natalya.

Scene 7
{Valeryan enters unnoticed.} His father notices him {begins to scold

*Throughout the volume, Tolstoy's comments are enclosed in curly brackets.

him} and lectures him briefly. Valeryan {says that his father cannot understand him}. A conversation about the new age. The Prince exits.

Scene 8
Valeryan is alone, he is sad, blames everyone and himself; he eagerly awaits his brother whom he has not seen for fifteen years.

Scene 9
The Princess returns with Lyolya, who just arrived. Valeryan is perturbed and he tells Lyolya why he cannot love her. Lyolya says that she does not love him very much either and is happy about that. The Princess and Lyolya exit.

Scene 10
Enter Ivan Ilich. Valeryan relates his sorrow to him and his story with the peasant women. Ivan Ilich does not understand and through his remarks insults him. They exit.

Scene 11
Enter Anatoly with Ivan Ilich. {Valeryan is happy, his frankness insults his brother.} Ivan Ilich says that there is a rich match. Anatoly says that he has come for the money. {Valeryan thinks that that is how one should be.}

Scene 12
Enter the Prince, Princess, and Lyolya. The Prince asks about Petersburg and is angry with his acquaintances, and advises Anatoly to do something useful. Anatoly haughtily slights the Princess and Lyolya. He also insults Ivan Ilich.

Scene 13
Enter Volodya and Natalya. They are servile, afraid for themselves. Anatoly frightens them with books, and the Prince takes his part. All exit.

Scene 14
Anatoly is alone, enter Valeryan, a scene of frankness and discord. Valeryan's despair.

ACT II
(in Volodya's room and office)

Scene 1
Volodya, Natalya, Pashenka, the housemaid are dining. A conversation about the young master, about the old man.

Scene 2
Peasant women and men enter, bow deeply. Pashenka asks forgiveness for one of the peasants and does needlepoint. They wait for the master, he comes to check the books. Volodya, Natalya, and the peasants exit.

Scene 3
Pashenka alone, she thinks it is a misfortune to be pretty, once she even found Valeryan at her door, but it is Anatoly that she has to attract.

Scene 4
Enter Anatoly, touches her.

Scene 5
Enter Volodya with books, he is politely sarcastic, but Anatoly is practical. Volodya gets caught; Anatoly reproves him severely and threatens him. Volodya is servile. Natalya eavesdrops, intervenes, and lets it be felt that she has authority. Anatoly exits.

Scene 6
Natalya is indignant, talks about letters of exchange[3] and her rights. {Just wait till the master dies.}

Scene 7
Change of scene {the drawing room}. The father's study. {The Princess and Valeryan. Valeryan does not answer questions, the Princess tries to persuade him to marry, Valeryan says that one such freak like himself is enough, the Princess does not understand him and says that she is rich, he knows.} Anatoly tells his father about Volodya's swindling, his father gives in, exits, Valeryan comes with L [?].[4]

Scene 8

Anatoly {becomes obsequious, makes inquiries} makes fun of his brother; the Princess laughs {cheerfully. Anatoly explains his situation to her, laden with debts, wife [?] is horrified}.

Scene 9

Enter the Prince from a walk with Lyolya and Ivan Ilich. Anatoly courts and is successful immediately. {The Princess hints to the Prince, he becomes angry and insults her.} Valeryan is in despair. {Anatoly tells his father about the mess. Valeryan is dead in his father's mind.} All exit except the old man.

Scene 9⁵

Enter Natalya, she begins to gossip {and relates how Valeryan is honest and gave away his aunt's share, whereas Anatoly squandered it long ago}. The old man is indignant with Anatoly—he is only for Pashe [?].

Scene 10

{Enter Anatoly, the Prince. The Princess speaks for her son, the Prince reviles Anatoly.}

ACT III
(in the Prince's study)

Scene 1

Anatoly and the Prince. Anatoly wants to get married.[6]

Scene 1

At Volodya's. Natalya complains to her friend, the foreman's wife, that their young mistress has ruined everything, that things are bad for her and her husband, and that their letters of exchange have been taken away.

Scene 2

Volodya relates that Anatoly is leaving and will probably speak with his father.

Change of scene. Scene 3
Valeryan and Ivan Ilich. Valeryan is sad, overly frank, and drinks—exits.

Scene 4
Anatoly, Lyolya, the Princess, the Prince, leave-taking, breakfast. Anatoly brazenly pursues an answer. Father Nata [?]. The Prince says that he owes Volodya twenty thousand.

Scene 5
Enter Natalya and Volodya, she brazenly intervenes, a coarse scene, Volodya, thoroughly moved, cries.

Scene 6
{Enter Valeryan, drunk, and Ivan Ilich.} Drinking hand to fist, a tragic Valeryan tells everyone the truth. The Prince cries, is angry, is remorseful, and exits. {Anatoly makes ready to depart.} Valeryan asks forgiveness from his father, explains why he lives here, that he has to love someone. It makes no difference that his life has been wasted. Anatoly is composed, asks whether or not he should take leave of his father. It is better not to, and he exits. Evgeniya [?][7] runs in and says to Valeryan that she loves him. The End.

A Practical Man

A Comedy in Three Acts

Prince Osip Ivanovich Kolomin,
  50
Princess Natalya Dmitrievna
  his wife, 45
Prince Anatoly [Anatolinka]
  Osipych
  their son, a Lieutenant in the
  Guards, 24
Prince Valeryan [Volinka]
  Osipych
  their other son, not in any
  service, 22
Olga [Olinka] Fyodorovna
  Versina
  a girl of 18; the daughter of
  wealthy neighbors
Volodya [Vladimir Petrovich,
  Volodka]
  the Prince's steward, a freeman,
  a merchant of the second guild,
  48

Natalya
  his wife, 37
Pashenka
  her sister, 20
General Dikov
  the Princess's brother
Ivan Ilich Pugalov
  a distant relative who lives in
  the Prince's home, 40
Egorka
  a servant
Peasant men and women

The action takes place at Prince
Kolomin's estate.

ACT I

The set depicts the drawing room of a wealthy country home. A round table in front of the sofa is set for tea. The samovar, coffee pot, basket for biscuits, and creamer are silver. A door to the study is to the right, a door to the bedroom is to the left, and there is a door directly into the garden.

SCENE 1

IVAN ILICH (*stands by the window smoking the very end of a cigar, continually looking over at the door to the left, and in his hands he holds a sealed letter*). A letter from Anatolinka—from Anatolinka (*looks at the middle*) in French! Can't make out a thing! I'd really like to know what he writes. His whole family, you know, they're my benefactors. Why shouldn't I be interested? Volodka was saying that he's in town already; he'll be here today. You know, I used to carry that Anatolinka around, I'd even pull him by the hair, but now Anatolinka has likely already become quite the Your Excellency. He'll come and'll suddenly say: get out of here, Ivan Ilich! Why's he sponging on us? Look, Ivan Ilich, get on the ball. (*He burns his fingers on the cigar.*) Ach, I don't feel like throwing it away, but the Princess'll walk in, and she'll start blustering again over the cigar. But the Princess is alright, you can adjust to her disposition, but now Anatolinka is coming, so wise up, Ivan Ilich. The main thing, if you start drinking, you're done for. I'll bear up to his disposition, and I'll tell him all about Volodya's affairs; that I, I'll say, though I'm not as smart as some Bruce,[1] I served my Tsar no worse than any other guy, and it's eighteen years I've been keeping your father calm, I don't ask for anything, and I could serve you honestly, sincerely, because I've gotten used to your family like my own. And why shouldn't I be the steward. Even colonels manage estates. If you'd set a salary for me, say a thousand roubles, then I'll take care of things properly. (*Enter the* PRINCESS. IVAN ILICH *disperses the smoke through the window, throws out the stub, and walks up to the* PRINCESS *and kisses her hand.*) A good morning to you, Princess-ma'am. Did you sleep well? For some reason the dogs were barking a lot last night by the greenhouse, didn't they disturb you?

PRINCESS. Good morning, my man. You've smelled everything up again with your black cigar. Who's that letter from?

IVAN ILICH. From Prince Anatoly Osipych, Princess. Vladimir Petrovich delivered it, he said that Anatoly Osipych stopped in town on some business matters for two hours; he'll be here for dinner.

PRINCESS (*reads the letter*). He'll definitely be here today, did you hear, Ivan Ilich?

IVAN ILICH. Of course I did, I'm happy. He'll be a joy and comfort to you.

PRINCESS (*pours the tea*). Oh, how you've smelled everything up with that tobacco. How many times do I have to tell you to smoke in the garden, on the porch.

IVAN ILICH (*waves his hands*). You're right, it does smell bad. It's the direction of the wind, Princess, I was actually smoking in the garden. I'm so filled with joy I've even quite lost my wits—because I love your home just like my own. Now Vladimir and Natalya are not very happy. (*Lowering his voice.*) He was telling me, Princess-ma'am, that Anatoly Osipych isn't coming for your pleasure, that the Prince's health is bad, that there's nowhere to put him. He knows what's what, ma'am. When the Prince, Anatoly Osipych, like a clever man, really goes into the farming business, then all sorts of things'll come to light. It's already time for Vladimir Petrovich to stop abusing all his benefits—he's made himself a fortune; but, you know, forgive me Princess, up to now you've not been the mistress in the house but he has. The neighbors are saying, and even the peasants are saying, that the masters are not the Prince, not the Princess, but Volodka and Natalya. Yesterday the Zaitsovs were telling me: "Believe us, Ivan Ilich," they said, "we love and respect the Princess, and one couldn't help loving such an angel, but I'll tell you the truth, Natalya's the mistress in the house."

PRINCESS. Take your cup and stop gossiping, please. You know I loathe gossip.

IVAN ILICH. The weather has settled for awhile. Remember, the Prince even made fun of me, of my predicting everything. Like it says in Bruce,[2] if in the same year the sign of the Lion and Capricorn align, it'll be a fine summer. And that's how it is, just as I said.

PRINCESS. Some day you'll lose your mind over Bruce's calendar. Have you seen my husband?

IVAN ILICH. I was by his door, Princess, Natalya was with him. The Prince asked her to clean the comb. I think he had a bad night.

PRINCESS. Why didn't you go in? Was he really busy?

IVAN ILICH. I just didn't, I didn't dare disturb. How good these biscuits are that Zakhar has begun to make now. They were saying something there about Anatoly Osipych. I heard Natalya's voice.

PRINCESS. What were they saying?

IVAN ILICH. Natalya was chattering something, she's very displeased that Anatoly Osipych is coming, but I didn't catch it, she was saying something about his depenses,[3] but I don't remember.

PRINCESS. You aren't able to relate anything, you always just make up some strange words. Have you seen Volinka?

IVAN ILICH. I have, Princess, he's in the garden by the greenhouse, still reading books.

PRINCESS (*rings, enter* SERVANT). Go to the garden, ask Valeryan Osipych to tea; say, "the Princess asked me to inform you: do you want the Prince to be angry again that you are not in time for tea?"(*Exit* SERVANT.) Ah, my God, what a strange sort that Volinka is! I'll tell you, Ivan Ilich, he costs me many tears.

IVAN ILICH. I see everything, Princess, and I understand your feelings and my heart bleeds, seeing you pained. But, it can be said, he's singularly kindhearted and is also unusually smart. There is one thing—his character; he doesn't want to serve, and this aggravates his dad, but he really does love and feel sorry for you. He understands everything. We often talk together, and it even brings him to tears. "I can't serve, I can't do anything, and I feel awfully sorry for my momma, I'm disgusted with all this," he says, "because I..."

PRINCESS. Well there's one thing that I often think, we have to... But one can't tell you anything, you'll spill it immediately to my husband and to him.

IVAN ILICH (*offended*). Ah, dear Princess, it's not right of you to hurt me, that I would really give away someone's secrets. Only scoundrels do that, you know. How could you think that of me?

PRINCESS. Well, see to it then, don't tattle, you know how I hate gossip. I'll tell you because he's frank with you. You find out from him and tell me. I want to marry him to Olinka Zhitova.[4] Now it seems to me that he's not indifferent to her. She would completely correct his character. A woman's influence is the main thing for a man. You lead him on to this conversation, and then tell me how he feels, because I, his mother, just don't get it. Now it seems he's in love, now...

IVAN ILICH (*listening with increased attention*). That thought, dear Princess, is from God. That's a good thing. He must be married without fail. The Zhitovs have a fine estate, and he's really in love—he's frank with me—so that it's simply amours.[5] It's only a matter of setting him straight, nothing more. The Zhitovs have only one daughter and, apart from the local one, an estate in the Saratov district with eight hundred souls, an estate, they say, that's lined with gold.

ACT II

Enter the PRINCE.

An Uncle's Blessing

A Comedy in Two Acts

Lydia Nikanorovna Eniseyeva
*over 30, dressed in the very
latest fashion, always speaks
French and smokes cigars*

Pyotr Fyodorych Eniseyev
*her husband, over 40,
dressed fashionably and
modestly; fat, good-natured,
choleric person*

Jean Moslosky
*22; has not finished a
course of study anywhere;
very fashionably and colorfully
dressed, a full head of hair,
wears a monocle; Lydia's lover.
[The surname of this character
changes in the play to
Moslosskoy.]*

Semyon Nikolaevich Klyaksin
*nearing 60, an important
official, a modest, self-confident,
elderly courtier with smoothly
shorn grey hair; Lydia's uncle
and lover*

Prince Shervanshidze
*19, very handsome, in Georgian
dress; speaks Russian poorly,
with a particular Georgian
accent on the vowels*

Olga Mikhailovna
*16, a relative of Pyotr
Fyodorych, who just arrived
from the country*

Anatoly Nikanorovich Latskan
*25, Lydia's brother and Olga's
fiancé; handsome infantry
officer with long hair and a
lorgnette*

Anna Nikanorovna Latskan
*22, his sister and Lydia's;
unmarried*

Katerina Fedotovna
*40, Olga's serf, part-maid,
part-nannie*

Count Kukshev
60, an old bachelor

The action takes place in Moscow.

The set depicts Lydia's boudoir. There are doors to the right and in the middle of the room.

Scene 1

Lydia and Moslosskoy speak about love. Lydia says she does not love him any longer. George Sand,[1] one has to be frank. She loves the Georgian Prince. He is already jealous over the old man [Semyon Nikolaevich].

Scene 2

Olga enters with Katerina Fedotovna. She is shamed over her dress and is to have her hair cropped. She gets angry and exits. They continue to speak about love and jealousy over Olga.

Scene 3

Husband [Pyotr Fyodorych] enters. He says that that is how things are nowadays, he understands, but why slight the old man, he is needed. Lydia says that he is right, that he is her best friend, but nevertheless she is suffering because of her love for the Georgian Prince and her jealousy. Thus, marry her [Olga] to her [Lydia's] brother. Her brother is a fool, he only wants to get married. She [Olga], it seems, is also in love. Besides, they should go abroad together, their affairs are in bad shape.

Scene 4

Latskan arrives, they mock him, sneer, and tell him to get married. He agrees. They walk around the room.

Scene 5

{They are left alone, he declares his love.} T arrives. He is angry, scolds M. The husband calms them. He reproaches the young lady on the side, gives her money, he says, just to find out.

Scene 6

Latskan announces that he has proposed. Everyone congratulates him. She [Olga] must go to her uncle for his blessing.

Scene 7

Enter Georgian Prince. Lydia chases everyone out and wants to explain George Sand to him, and that Olga is getting married {he turns argument against her}. She [Lydia] says: she is dear to him and you are repugnant, one cannot love two women.

ACT II

Scene 1

The Count's village. He is drinking tea, Katerina Fedotovna comes. He tells her that things are bad. She herself does not know how this happened.

Scene 2

Olga proudly says that she loves the portrait. He [Pyotr] is rude. Why have you [Olga] come—the blessing is nonsense, money. She gets angry: she says that everything is over. He is remorseful, calms her. She says that she thinks she is in love.

Scene 3

Katerina Fedotovna calms her with flattery.

Scene 4

She charms the Count, decides to test him.

ACT III

Lydia's boudoir; husband, two lovers, and Latskan in the corner; she is sad; the Prince promised to come. Pr. speaks about Olga's arrival; husband was at her place and relates that she did not say anything about money. She comes, is cold, silent about money. Off to one side they speak with Latskan about kisses, they inquire about the money, coldness. The Georgian Prince comes, runs after Olga. Lydia quarrels with her, talks about her fiancé. Olga and Prince turn her argument against her. {The old man distracts her and all the others. The husband remains with Olga, asks why she has changed, about the money, she tells him.} Lydia becomes furious, talks about the money, a scene. The Georgian Prince offers his hand, she sends him away.

Free Love

A Comedy in Two Acts

Lydia [Lydi, Lily] Andrevna
  Shchurina
  *nearing 30, in striking attire
  and hairstyle*
Dmitry Sergeich Shchurin
  *her husband, nearing 40;
  suffered a stroke, very fat
  and lazy*
Kapitolina Andrevna
  *her sister, 25, unmarried,
  dressed as eccentrically as her
  older sister*
Olga [Olinka, Olin]
  *Shchurin's niece, a 19-year-old
  young lady who just arrived
  from the country*
Maslovskoy
  *22, a lean dandy with a
  monocle and wearing numerous
  pendants; Lydia's lover*
His Excellency Ivan Nikanorych
  Latskan
  *nearing 60, an elderly man
  of some importance, polite and
  worldly; Lydia's uncle and lover*
Lieutenant Colonel Kuleshenko
  35, recently back from a war

Prince Chivchivchidze
  *18, very handsome, dressed in a
  Georgian outfit; speaks Russian
  somewhat inaccurately and
  places particular emphasis on
  the vowels*
Katerina Fedotovna
  *around 40, serf housemaid and
  Olga's nannie; came with Olga
  from the country*
The Shchurins' hired footman

*The action takes place in Moscow,
in the Shchurins' very lavishly and
pretentiously appointed home.*

ACT I

The set depicts LYDIA's *boudoir. The room is covered in silk. An opaque lamp hangs from the middle of the ceiling, and there are a large and small sofa, a mirror, a door to the right, and a second door in the center. On one wall, on a tapestry, hang pistols and daggers, and in front of the large sofa lies a bear skin. A Newfoundland dog is on the small sofa. In the corner, there is a cage with a parrot.*

S C E N E 1

LYDIA (*alone, is lying on the large sofa, clothed in a red nightgown and ermine slippers, and smoking a cigar; on the table next to her is a bottle of wine*). That sweet savage...my Teverino[1] ... Yes, I really love him, and I'll tell the whole world that I love him. I remember how Maslovskoy brought him to me at that ball and asked me, jokingly, not to fall in love with him. But I fell in love, and fell passionately in love, because I couldn't help it—that Georgian outfit that fit him so well, that southern, passionate face, that beautiful hair... No, I can't spend this evening without him, and I must tell him how much I love him. I've always just said "I love you" to the people I love, because I'm proud of this feeling, so this savage little Prince has to be hugged and kissed in front of everyone for him to feel my love and allow him to express his; and I'll do it. Thank God I've long since risen above the preconceptions of the throng. (*Raises herself to the table, moves over an inkwell and papercase and writes.*) My dear, sweet Prince... I expect you this evening... (*Rings.*) I expect you this evening... I hope that in Georgia, too, one complies with the requests of ladies... (*Enter* SERVANT.) Wait a moment... (*Writes in silence.*) No, he won't understand, it's better to send my husband for him. (*Addressing the* SERVANT.) Where's Dmitry Sergeich?

SERVANT. He's resting, madam.

LYDIA. Wake him and have him come here quickly.

SERVANT. Yes, madam. (*Exits.*)

LYDIA (*tears up the note she began, takes a sip of wine and loses herself in thought*). No...he loves me, too, I feel it... (*Becomes thoughtful again and smiles.*) We'll be alone here this evening...perhaps a moment of true happiness. There's one thing...my unbearable uncle will disturb us again, he'll come with his antiquated endearments... (SHCHURIN *enters, shakes so as to awaken himself completely. Not looking at him,* LYDIA *extends her hand to him.*) How are you, my dear, what were you doing?

SHCHURIN (*sits down on a chair next to her*). I was resting. You sent for me, Lily?

LYDIA. Shchurin, will you do me a favor?

SHCHURIN. Anything you wish, Lily.

LYDIA. Do you know where Prince Chivchivchidze[2] lives?

SHCHURIN. You mean that handsome little fellow, Lily? No, I don't.

LYDIA. Well, find him, only go now and tell him that I wish to see him here without fail this evening. Listen, Shchurin, be nice as usual, after all I seldom ask you for anything, and leave you completely free. Do go.

SHCHURIN. Lily, please don't be angry at what I'm going to say to you. I, too, seldom tell you anything. I respect you too much and value your candor. But, *cher* Lily, don't invite him today; you know why.

LYDIA. No I don't.

SHCHURIN. It seems, we've gotten to know each other in ten years. You've seen that I've never, not once, allowed myself to be jealous of you. Believe me, I understand as well as you the completely ridiculous, dishonest side of jealousy in our time. I know that love must be free, and that candor is more noble than all else. But Lily, *ma chère*, now I'm not asking for myself that you don't invite the Georgian Prince today, and that you should be more careful with him in general. It would be too ridiculous and stupid if I were jealous of you, like a boy. I ask this for you. You know, your uncle is a man not of this age, he doesn't look at this the way I do...

LYDIA. Oh, my God! How ridiculous you are, Shchurin! And who told my uncle to fall in love with me.

SHCHURIN. Well, of course...

LYDIA. So what am I to do? His senile passion amused me at first, but I'm long since tired of it. Who's stopping him from loving me like a friend, like a niece, but jealousy, requests, endearments...I can't and don't want to constrain myself for anyone.

SHCHURIN. Lily, you're still a complete child... Think about how much this man has done for us, and how much he can do and will do if you yourself don't antagonize him. You don't care to know about our means; but, if not for him, we would long since have had nothing to live on. Just think, how much more he can still do for us with his passion for you. Let's assume that this passion is ridiculous and a burden to you; nevertheless, you must encourage it. Just think about it, Lily, you have children.

LYDIA (*irritated*). You're always right.

SHCHURIN. So, what's there to do?

LYDIA. I know that you're right, but what am I to do? You know me, I can't pretend and hide my feelings. (*Heatedly.*) I love the Prince, like no one I've ever loved before! For him I'm prepared to give up everything—the children, everything in the world. And you want me to sacrifice this sacred, lofty feeling for your financial calculations. (*With pride.*) No, Shchurin, you still don't know me and don't want to understand!

SHCHURIN (*calmly*). Lily, I know you, I value you; ten years worth of friendly relations should have convinced you of that, but be sensible, my dear. It's already three years that I, with pleasure, have been witnessing your relations with Maslovskoy, and I know that he's our best friend. This past winter you fell for that hero, the Colonel, and I didn't say anything either, because you, as usual, were sincere and honest in your infatuation, and it didn't harm anyone. But now do remember what you owe your uncle, what we can still expect from him. We have to treat him with care; but in his presence you flirt so carelessly with that Prince. Two days ago I saw how your uncle's face changed, and he left immediately after you tore into Olinka, and then led the Prince off to the greenhouse and locked the doors. Be careful, if not for me then for yourself and your children. That's all I ask of you, be sensible.

LYDIA. I told you that I'm in love and I can't be sensible—especially when I see that niece of yours, Olga, whom you brought here, God knows why, flirting with the Prince. That arouses my passion even more, I'll do a lot of foolish things, and you want me to be sensible. And why did you bring that Olga here? Is it something sensible, too? Send her back.

SHCHURIN. Precisely, sensibleness again requires this. However painful this may be for me, Lily, nevertheless I have to contradict you for a second time. Olinka is a good girl; true, she's provincial, backward, but she's my closest relative, she's an orphan, and, most important, without her three thousand a year, we couldn't remain any longer in Moscow, I assure you.

LYDIA. Well, wonderful, all's wonderful and true, but do go to the Prince and bring him back. I ask you only this one thing.

SHCHURIN (*with a stern, threatening expression*). Lily... (*Enter* MASLOVSKOY.)

SCENE 2

THE SAME *and* MASLOVSKOY.

SHCHURIN (*not rising, gives him his hand*). *Bonjour, cher.* Maybe you'd help me persuade this scatterbrain: perhaps you'll be more convincing than I've been.

LYDIA (MASLOVSKOY *kisses her extended hand as he sits down by her feet on the sofa*). No, he understands me better and he'll do what I ask. He loves me and is therefore generous but not sensible. (*She utters the last word disdainfully.*)

MASLOVSKOY. I'll do anything, especially today (*looking at her tenderly*) when you're so charming... (*She squeezes his hand.*) You know you lost the bet—Kuleshenko really wears a hairpiece—I found out. For sure. (*Lowering his voice.*) So I have a right to kiss your little foot...

SHCHURIN (*stands up and walks over to the parrot*). Hey polly! Polly! Polly! Yoo hoo.

LYDIA (*smiling*). Yes, but first you still have to fulfill my request. Go now, find Prince Chivchivchidze wherever, and bring him to me this evening without fail. Without fail, do you hear! That's what I want.

MASLOVSKOY. Are you still in love with him?

LYDIA. No, Maslovskoy! I'm not in love—in love—that's somehow stupid, banal, and I don't love him the way I do you, but it's something both more and less. I'm certain I know this much in advance, that I'll be fed up with this young savage in three days, and I'll again be wholly yours. But now I love him and want him so passionately that I think I'll die if I don't see him. He wasn't here yesterday, and in the evening I took opium and, my God, what delight! And now I've already prepared a pastille again for today, if he doesn't come. I know that you'll do this for me, you're my best friend and you're so gentle that you can understand all the nuances of a woman's feeling.

MASLOVSKOY (*has been looking at her with a tender smile during her entire monologue*). Yes, Lydi, I understand you, but don't forget that although I'll always do everything that I can for your happiness, at times it's a painful sacrifice for me. I have completely committed myself to you forever, without demanding anything from you and accepting with gratitude what you give me. You gave me your friendship, you gave me the right to speak to you about my love, and I'm happy. But in my heart I'd still like to have all of you, your friendship as well as your passions. Didn't I suffer when I brought you Kuleshenko, (*ironically*) that hero of Sevastopol, who got himself a bank draft there for ten thousand. But all your passions, and even your mistakes, are sacred to me. I never tried to disenchant you. You became disenchanted yourself, but still just for a while, you were happy, and I was gladdened and suffered, seeing you happy. This time, too, I'm glad that I can bring you happiness through this charming young savage, but don't ask me what's here. (*Points to his heart.*) If I dared to be jealous of you, I'd be jealous of you not for these momentary impulses, which only excite my love more, and after which you return to me all the more seductive, but I'd be jealous of you on account of your old man, Unc, as you call him, who's always asserting some sort of right over you, and to whom you seemingly give that right. That's whom I hate. You remember, the twenty-eighth of May, when I first came to love you, I bought this ring with poison and told you that if I should ever cease being something to you, I'll have nothing to do in this world... And your relations with that old man frequently make me glance at this ring. If not I but he were to become your indispensable friend, I'd not think for a moment...... (*Pretends that he is swallowing the ring.*)

LYDIA (*squeezes his hand*). *Cher ami* !.......... So you'll bring him today?

MASLOVSKOY (*rising*). Immediately! (*Nodding his agreement. Addresses*

SHCHURIN.) Dmitry Sergeich! I asked a certain Gentleman to sort out your affair at the Council—I was promised.

SHCHURIN. I know that you're a splendid person. So, did you talk to her?...

MASLOVSKOY. Yes... I... (*Goes up to* LYDIA.)

SHCHURIN (*rises and also goes up to* LYDIA, *who does not listen to him and speaks at the same time*). He also agrees, Lily, that you have to treat a man like your uncle with care. Who's arguing, you like this Princelet like a child, but you have to be sensible.

LYDIA. Maslovskoy! You come, too. Come over here. If he comes today, I want to talk about many things with him, explain many things to this sweet savage. I'm afraid he'll shun me because, with his Oriental Caucasian[3] ideas, he fancies that my husband will knife him, that I'm a married woman, et cetera. Olga will hinder me. Please be really big-hearted, occupy her this evening, and Unc, your friend, if he comes. Otherwise I won't have a moment's peace.

MASLOVSKOY. I'll do better: I'll bring the brave Colonel so as to occupy Olga, whom you wrongfully fear, and we'll get Unc to the card table.

SHCHURIN (*together with* MASLOVSKOY). Now that's great and smart.

LYDIA. You're delightful! Do go.

MASLOVSKOY. No, do you know what I thought of? The brave Colonel—may I now speak freely about him?—is horribly dumb, and his ten-thousand-rouble bank draft has confused him completely. It's not enough for him alone to rent boxes in the dress circle and carriages, his dream is to marry whomever. We should marry him to Olinka, he'll be perfectly happy, and you'll be rid of the two of them at once. How's that for an idea!

LYDIA. Marvelous. In half an hour I'll have Olga in love with the brave Colonel. She's a passionate girl, like all provincial girls, with antiquated ideas about love, and none too clever...

SHCHURIN (*together with* LYDIA). Yes, she's also a nice girl, and I'm responsible for her. God knows if he'll make her happy.

LYDIA (*addressing* SHCHURIN). No one's speaking to you, you didn't want to do what I asked...

OLGA *enters from a side door. She is dressed in a white, muslin skirt and* black lace wrap, and has a braid around her head. She curtsies to MASLOVSKOY. A door opens behind her and KATERINA FEDOTOVNA gives her a kerchief, and puts her dress in order. MASLOVSKOY bows to the ladies, shakes SHCHURIN's hand, and exits.

SCENE 3

SHCHURIN, LYDIA, OLGA, and KATERINA FEDOTOVNA.

LYDIA (takes OLGA by the hand and, raising herself, looks her over). Olin! You're terribly pretty, fresh, but, don't be angry with me, terribly provincial. What an outfit!

SHCHURIN (looking her over). Yes, my dear, you're sweet, but in today's society there are so many conventions... It's all...

OLGA (blushing). So am I ridiculous? What's wrong with my dress?...

LYDIA (rising). Everything, ma chère. In the first place, that wrap, it's too dressy and spoils your waist. Better put on my ermine one.

SHCHURIN. I'll have it brought to you now.

LYDIA. Then, there's that dress that's been washed thirty times—maids, you know, wear the like. Well, it's still not that bad. Let's see your shoes.

OLGA (shows her foot). What about my shoes?

LYDIA (laughing). It's very nice that you don't care, but who wears such shoes? Weren't you brought any? At least put mine on, but they'll be small on you. (Puts her foot next to hers.) Yes, they're small.

OLGA. Will there really be that many guests that you dress me so?

LYDIA. The Colonel, who is very...

An Infected Family

A Comedy in Five Acts

Ivan [Jean] Mikhailovich
   [Mikhalych] Pribyshev
   a landowner, 50
Marya Vasilevna
   his wife, 48
Lyubov [Lyubochka, Lyuba,
   Lyubinka] Ivanovna
   their daughter, an 18-year-old
   young lady
Katerina [Katenka, Katinka,
   Katya] Matveyevna Dudkina
   their niece, unmarried, 26
Pyotr [Petrusha, Petinka, Petya,
   Petrushka] Ivanovich
   their son, a high-school boy, 15
Marya [Mashka] Isaevna
   former nannie, at present the
   housekeeper; family friend, of
   serf origin, 45

Aleksey Pavlovich Tverdynskoy
   a 22-year-old young man living
   with the Pribyshevs, from whom
   he receives room and board; [the
   student—Pyotr Ivanovich's
   teacher] from a family of clerics
Anatoly [Tolya, Anatole]
   Dmitrievich [Dmitrich]
   Venerovsky
   an excise official, 35
Foreman
Overseer
Footman [Sashka, Aleksandr
   Vasilich]
Peasants

The action takes place at the
Pribyshevs' estate.

The dramatis personae given here is for Act I.

ACT I

Morning. The parlor of a rural landowner's home. There is a round table in front of the sofa. A tea and coffee service are on the table.

SCENE 1

The NANNIE *is knitting a stocking. Standing, she pours out the tea;* MARYA VASILEVNA *is sitting at the table, drinking tea.*

NANNIE. Hand me the cup, I'll fill it. What are you doin'? Really, you're not drinkin', just foolin' around. (*Takes the cup.*)

MARYA VASILEVNA (*with hurt feeings*). Now, Nannie, wait a minute, I haven't finished yet. And why are you yelling, as though I were a child? Really! There, now you can fill it. (*Hands over the cup.*)

NANNIE. I'm waitin', waitin', waitin', waitin'. It's eleven o'clock already, and I've still not served half the gentry. You'll be finished with tea, but the old master, and the stoodent and Petrusha'll be comin'.

MARYA VASILEVNA. What stoodent? It's student.

NANNIE. To me he's a stoodent, and I don't like him, he's a sloppy person. A good-for-nothin'.

MARYA VASILEVNA. But I pity him, Nannie.

NANNIE. What's there to pity. Has he ever said a kind word to anyone? He's been in the house for over a month and the only thing he's done is sneer (*mimicking him*). It seems that he, together with that niece of yours, has ridiculed everyone. What's more the maids can't get rid of him. He's all over them, the slob. I've already prepared Dunyasha: "If he starts pesterin' you, you smack him across the face so that he comes to dinner with a bruise. Let 'em ask how he got it." And besides, what's this business? Do we really have to supply him? All the beddin' is ours.

MARYA VASILEVNA. Oh, Nannie, what a person you are! Just think, he is, you know, alone, young, and poor. I really wonder, why is he so thin?

NANNIE. He'll certainly fatten up! He'll soon come with Petrusha and drink his fill. Then'll come Katerina Matveyevna, our golden one, with a book... I'll serve 'em, thank God, and as soon as I've cleared the table off, again coffee! Breakfast! Spindlelegs'll show up!

MARYA VASILEVNA. What names you always have, Nannie! Who's this spindlelegs?

NANNIE. Why Anatoly Dmitrich, Lyubochka's fiancé.

MARYA VASILEVNA. You talk such nonsense. What do you mean fiancé? The young man simply calls on her.

NANNIE. So you think that Nannie Marya's as dumb as they come. You'd suppose that I'd learned somethin' after thirty years of service upstairs. Do you think he comes here just for coffee—every blessed day, eleven miles from town? Not at all, ma'am! He comes cause he's figured out what Lyubochka's dowry'll be, that's for sure.

MARYA VASILEVNA. So that's how you think! First of all, he's not her fiancé, and secondly he's not one to be tempted by money. Anatoly Dmitrievich is not at all like that.

NANNIE. These days, ma'am, no one takes a bride without money, no matter how beautiful. Only, he's no prize as a groom. He's sort of run-of-the-mill, does somethin' or other with liquor, but nothin' special. Besides, I've asked around, not a good word about him. First of all he's stingy, then he's highfalutin.

MARYA VASILEVNA. What kind of word is that? How did you say it?

NANNIE. Highfalutin, ma'am. That's our way of sayin': I'm better than everyone, smarter than everyone, and everyone's a fool except me.

MARYA VASILEVNA. Now that's not true. He's a scholar, a writer. But what do you know!

NANNIE. I'm just sorry for Lyubochka, he's completely turned her head.

MARYA VASILEVNA. Perhaps it's not Lyubochka that he's courting but Katenka. So there!

NANNIE. What do you mean, I'm not so stupid to believe that. He was foolin' around a bit with Katerina Matveyevna, but that's all. She used to chase after him when she was still workin' as a governoress in Petersburg, but marry—he knows who'll bring the money and who won't, that's for sure.

MARYA VASILEVNA. Katenka did know him in Petersburg. You see bad in everyone.

NANNIE. But that's how it is, ma'am, as soon as they become governoresses, they wind up acting like governoresses. That's for certain. And that's how Katerina Matveyevna was.

MARYA VASILEVNA (*laughs and waves her hands*). Enough, nonsense.

NANNIE. And we've noticed that things are different in the house. The master's different, he's become meek, you've taken this stoodent as a teacher instead of the German, you've let Katerina Matveyevna have her way, and you've let all the kids get out of hand. Everything has changed, everything's different.

MARYA VASILEVNA. So, am I also different? You are stupid.

NANNIE. You're what you were, always kind. But the master, often makes me wonder… (*Is silent, shakes her head, and throws up her hands.*) What's happened? He's altogether a different person. In the past, as I remember, was there ever a day that Sashka the valett didn't get a beatin' while dressin' him? Was there ever an overseer that didn't get hauled down to the police?…

MARYA VASILEVNA. Well, the way you tell it… Was it really very good? It wasn't at all good.

NANNIE. But I'm not praisin' and not blamin'. The gentry was gentry, and it can't be otherwise. And what's surprisin'—how can a man of fifty change… What's this Tsar's paper, that one, the one that came out durin' the first week?…

MARYA VASILEVNA. Oh yes, you mean the Manifesto[1]—how ridiculous you are!

NANNIE (*resentfully*). Oh yeah, that's it, sure you know all about it, the one that drives house-serfs out in the cold in thanks for their service. Oh well, forget it! What was I talkin' about. Ever since then things started to change. More than anythin' else I'm really disgusted. I heard him the other day in front of Anatoly Dmitrich. You'll forgive me, ma'am, I always tell the truth. You can't change at fifty. He's only lost his importance. He just wants to show off, but he's still the same. The other day, he, in front of Anatoly Dmitrich, began to humor what's-his-name, the peasant, Kiryushka Deyev: he says "sir," that was to Kiryushka, "if you wish to work, do come." I heard it: what's goin' on? As if to a prince of some sort. I just spat.

THE SAME and KATERINA MATVEYEVNA.

NANNIE. Look at the beauty, how's she's got up!

KATERINA MATVEYEVNA (*shorthaired, wearing eyeglasses and a short dress, with a book under her arm; sits down at the table without curtsying, leans on her elbows, takes out a cigarette and begins to read; addresses* NANNIE *with exaggerated politeness*). May I request some tea, Marya Isaevna? (NANNIE *serves her tea in a glass.*)

NANNIE. At once, madam, at once. (*Aside.*) Now she's really surprised everyone. She didn't even say "bonzhur" to her auntie. Like she's too smart.

MARYA VASILEVNA. Nannie and I were talking about Anatoly Dmitrievich. She says he's courting Lyubochka, but I say you, Katenka. *Comment croyez vous?* What do you think? She's already calling him her fiancé.

KATERINA MATVEYEVNA (*looks up from her book, and speaks sternly with a gesture*). In his development and views on life Venerovsky is so far removed from the banality of our life that it is difficult for us to judge him.

MARYA VASILEVNA. So you think he'll not marry!

KATERINA MATVEYEVNA. Excuse me! This gentleman would marry only in the event that he should find a woman who has understood her objectives fully, and is emancipated in her way of living and thinking. Were he to meet such a woman—of which there are few—he might get the desire to experience life with her; and if in this experience both equal parties would consider themselves satisfied, he would unite with this woman or young lady, but never in marriage, as you understand it. This is all very simple and clear.

MARYA VASILEVNA. *Non, mais dites.* Now tell me, whom is he after, you or Lyubochka? I was just speaking with Nannie, she's such a fool, I had a good laugh...

KATERINA MATVEYEVNA. Nannie Marya Isaevna is older than you and addresses you very respectfully, but you address her in an overly familiar manner. What's more, you call her a fool. I consider this an insult to the dignity and freedom of a human being, and by virtue of this conviction find it necessary to express my thoughts to you. I know that you have the right to hold your own convictions, but that grates and disturbs me.

NANNIE (*mockingly*). Well, thanks much for standin' up for me. (*Addressing* MARYA VASILEVNA.) But you, you're happy to draw my life's blood out. You're a real bad woman...

MARYA VASILEVNA. No, why, Katinka, *je plaisante*, I love her. No, do give me your opinion—whom is he after? Huh? You or Lyubochka. *Je voudrais savoir votre opinion.*

KATERINA MATVEYEVNA. How am I going to explain my opinion? (*Brushes her hair back and lights a cigarette.*) *After me*—as you, so to say, figuratively express it, he could not be. I have made myself into an emancipated woman and, therefore, my relationship toward him is straightforward, just as it is toward any other person, sex and position notwithstanding. I find him to be an intelligent and modern person, and in his relationship toward me, he, naturally, has that measure of respect and empathy which, so to say... In a word, he and I have a good and straightforward relationship of mutual respect, and he finds relaxation with me after all the pettiness of the provincial, female, aristocratic mob with which he must socialize. But why you think that he, as you figuratively express it, is after Lyubov Ivanovna, is beyond me. Lyubov is far too underdeveloped, in fact she is not developed at all, and such a personality as Venerovsky could not have anything in common with her. The so-called pretty little face, that decent people have long since ceased to appreciate, has its place and significance in aesthetics, but Lyubov lacks that beauty.

NANNIE (*aside*). She hasn't cut her hair yet like you! You're a beauty!

KATERINA MATVEYEVNA. Classical beauty has nothing in common with matrimony, because one does not need rights to form impressions. That is clear. Therefore, I surmise that this gentleman is not at all interested in Lyubov Ivanovna and is hardly aware of the existence of Lyubov Ivanovna here. He enjoys conversing with a thinking person and, on the whole, he enjoys a conversation with me and the student, Aleksey Pavlovich. And so, I am of the opinion that he is neither a suitor nor a fiancé, and he will never be either a fiancé or a husband, or anything of the like that is senseless and degrading to the dignity of a man. And if you phrase the question as follows: which of the relationships here does he prize more, the one with me or with Lyubov Ivanovna, then I surmise it would be ridiculous even to answer such a question. I am his equal, but Lyuba is a child.

MARYA VASILEVNA. Now do you see, Nannie, how Katinka thinks!

NANNIE. Okay Katerina Matveyevna ma'am, we're dumb, so you make sense of it: Will he keep on comin' just like that?

KATERINA MATVEYEVNA. Why should he stop coming?

NANNIE. Because such people ought be schooled. That's how it used to be. If you call on a home where there are two eligible girls, then own up, which one are you proposin' to—if not, that's why there're these clubs to go to. Go as much as you like.

KATERINA MATVEYEVNA. Marya Isaevna, you cannot understand me. I told you that he comes to me; we will experience one another and if we will find...

NANNIE. By my dumb reasoning, Katerina Matveyevna ma'am, he's not goin' to experience nothin'. Lyubov Ivanovna's a pretty young lady and with her comes five hundred souls. But you're, after all, older, and he won't be tempted by thirty souls... Now the stoodent would.

KATERINA MATVEYEVNA (*heatedly*). Excuse me, excuse me. The student is young and underdeveloped for me. Excuse me. Another woman in my place might feel insulted, but I am above that. Lyubov Ivanovna is no match for him with her childish demands from life; he is aware of this as he himself has mentioned to me several times. That's for one. Secondly, you look at the matter from the wrong point of view. You will not understand me but, nevertheless, I will have my say and will try to speak more simply. For people of our temper only those means in life are permissible that are acquired through personal and honest labor. Believe me, people of our time consider all these estates to be only a delusive tie with obsolete ways of life. It is all the same to Venerovsky whether I should have a million or nothing if only our views on life are identical. If they are identical, then we can boldly enter into the fray.

NANNIE. Anyway, he won't propose to you but he will to Lyubov Ivanovna. You take five hundred souls, it's very identical to him, but thirty souls ain't so identical at all.

KATERINA MATVEYEVNA (*resentfully*). Excuse me, excuse me, all right. You say that I have thirty souls. Allow me to tell you that thanks to enlightenment no one has souls any more, and I never had any. I renounced my rights the very moment I came of age so that the shameful stamp of serfage lies not upon me.

NANNIE. So they were freed for money. But some didn't even get money.

KATERINA MATVEYEVNA. Excuse me please, excuse me. I do not know that, my uncle did it. Whether he did good or bad—I do not want to know this. I know what I had to do. (*Gesticulating and brushing back her hair.*) I renounced it, turned my back in horror and expiated the shame of my forebearers by suffering.

NANNIE. But he won't have you anyway, and he'll propose to Lyubochka, cuz...

MARYA VASILEVNA (*nervously*). Enough, Nannie, what a person you are! You'll drive anyone out of their mind.

KATERINA MATVEYEVNA. Excuse me, excuse me, all right. All this seems difficult and complicated to you. Your thoughts are on betrothal, Almighty God, and the like; however, the life of people who place themselves above the social web of prejudices is very simple. I will express my ideas to him and demand that sincerity which underlies all the impulses of an honorable personality.

NANNIE. Ach, Katerina Matveyevna ma'am! Lyubov Ivanovna has five hundred souls. Besides, he may fall in love.

KATERINA MATVEYEVNA (*completely perplexed*). Why would he fall in love with an undeveloped, insignificant girl but not fall in love with me?

NANNIE. Why? Here's why, ma'am—for goat's wool.

KATERINA MATVEYEVNA (*collecting her senses and pushing her hair back*). No, what am I doing! Lyubov, as you understand her, is a carnal attraction, and you are too undeveloped and too much of an animal to understand me. Please, I beg you, leave me alone. (*Leans on her elbows and reads.*)

MARYA VASILEVNA. Go, go away, Nannie. I'll pour the tea if someone comes.

NANNIE (*exiting*). She's shamed everyone. Everyone's an animal. I've been servin' for thirty years and no one ever called me an animal...

KATERINA MATVEYEVNA (*raises her head from the book*). Excuse me. Love is an honorable impulse only when both parties are equal, but you do not understand that. (*Silence, raising her head.*) Marya Vasilevna, I do not respect that woman. (*Continues reading.*)

SCENE 3

Enter IVAN MIKHAILOVICH.

IVAN MIKHAILOVICH. What's this, who don't you respect?

MARYA VASILEVNA. Nannie keeps on talking nonsense.

IVAN MIKHAILOVICH. Oh, she spits poison but is otherwise a good woman. (*Sits down at the table.*) Well, Marya Vasilevna, let's have some tea. I've been in the field since five and wore out two horses. But for all that, I've put things right. And they say you can't do anything with freed workers, imagine that! Yes you can, as long as you're everywhere and don't spare yourself. Yesterday half the field wasn't ploughed, the meadows weren't mowed, and there wasn't a single worker. When I took a hand in it, I talked my peasants into working, hired the freed ones, and threw in a bucket of vodka. Now look, things are in full swing. Vasily is a real good foreman, he's so capable, great, just great.

KATERINA MATVEYEVNA. Free labor cannot be unprofitable. That runs contrary to all the fundamental laws of political economy.

IVAN MIKHAILOVICH. That's right, and it's not right. If I'd saddle you and Anatoly Dmitrievich with this work, you wouldn't talk like that.

MARYA VASILEVNA. *Dites moi, mon cher Jean,* why do you keep on saying that things are better since the Manifesto? How are things better now that they all have left?

IVAN MIKHAILOVICH. Oh, that's the domestics.

MARYA VASILEVNA. I know about the domestics, that's understandable, but now even the peasants no longer work. I don't see what's so good about it.

IVAN MIKHAILOVICH. I've already explained to you maybe not a hundred but about fifty times that, according to the Manifesto, they have to work some days but not every day. That's the whole point.

MARYA VASILEVNA. Why then do they say that they've stopped working entirely? The other day everyone was saying that they were sent to work but didn't go. I don't understand that, *Jean.*

IVAN MIKHAILOVICH. If they didn't work at all, we'd long since have had nothing to eat. They just work less—but it's all legitimate and not arbitrary. Well, you won't understand.

MARYA VASILEVNA. So what's so good that they work less? That means it wasn't done properly. But don't get angry, *ne vous fâchez pas,* I just don't understand.

IVAN MIKHAILOVICH. Why should I get angry, it's obviously your fate, you know, not to understand anything. (*Takes a cup of tea and loses himself in thought.*) And where's Lyuba?

MARYA VASILEVNA. Early this morning she went to gather mushrooms with the girls.

IVAN MIKHAILOVICH. And Anatoly Dmitrievich still hasn't come or sent word?

MARYA VASILEVNA. Not yet. There's something I wanted to tell you, *Jean.* I heard that Anatoly Dmitrievich *veut faire la proposition à* Lyuba, wants to propose, as they say, to Lyubochka.

IVAN MIKHAILOVICH. Who did you hear it from?

MARYA VASILEVNA. *On dit.* That's what they're saying.

IVAN MIKHAILOVICH. Who's saying it? You sit between four walls, who could tell you. Well, so what that they talk.

MARYA VASILEVNA. I know my opinion means nothing to you. It's just that I heard he's not a nice person. What kind of occupation is dealing with liquor! But the main thing is that he's highfalutin. Please, *Jean,* think about this.

IVAN MIKHAILOVICH. What don't come into that head of yours! And where did you pick up those words? No, my dear, don't give me that nonsense. What's this highfalutin—where did you get that stupid word from.

MARYA VASILEVNA. Everyone talks that way.

IVAN MIKHAILOVICH. What don't pop into that noggin! Who told you this nonsense? Ah, my dear, it's not for us to judge this man. Any father would consider it an honor to be related to such a man. Besides, I can't stand guesswork or matchmaking. It's in God's hands whatever he happens to be, and there's nothing for us to question. He's an outstanding man, a writer. And he's certainly not marrying for money. That's for sure.

MARYA VASILEVNA. No one is saying this. *J'ai mon opinion,* that's my own opinion.

IVAN MIKHAILOVICH. Well, then listen: in the first place Anatoly Dmitrievich is a progressive, modern person, a man of intellect and learning, a writer who, perhaps, all of Russia knows. These days, my dear, that's better than a general's rank. Secondly, he has an excellent and honest occupation—in the new excise service—and an income of two thousand. All doors are open to such a man, if only he wants it. That he has peculiar ways and all is another matter. He's not a polished man but, you know, at least he's truly unselfish. When this man marries, it won't be for money. Any girl would be happy with him even if she didn't have a thing.

MARYA VASILEVNA. But they're saying that he's stingy.

IVAN MIKHAILOVICH. So you're off again! I'm telling you, a truly unselfish man. That's already proven.

MARYA VASILEVNA. But they're saying that he's figured out to the last kopeck what her dowry'll be.

IVAN MIKHAILOVICH. Katenka, maybe you can explain to her that Anatoly Dmitrievich is not that kind of man.

KATERINA MATVEYEVNA. Both Marya Vasilevna and Marya Isaevna have their own convictions. What I find most odd is the basis on which one may accuse a man, who has not given any cause, of the vilest intentions. This gentleman's entire life proves that his only interest is the common good. If this gentleman were to contemplate uniting with a woman, his foremost condition would be independence, personal as well as financial.

IVAN MIKHAILOVICH (*lost in thought; silence*). Yes, even though it's difficult for the likes of us older folk to change our old-fashioned ways, one must give the new generation its due, for all the excesses and frivolity of youth. Yes.

KATERINA MATVEYEVNA (*looking up from her book*). From all that you have said, I share your conviction in this one thing. Progress inevitably sheds light on the most obdurate conditions of life.

IVAN MIKHAILOVICH (*after a brief silence*). Yes, free labor keeps on progressing, and progressing. It's difficult to deal with the workers. But, that's all right, things'll be fine... Just let me handle this redemption business and finish up with the peasants. Then, only relationships with landowners will remain. And really, that's good, yes.

MARYA VASILEVNA. Will redemption really be better, *Jean*? I think it would be.

IVAN MIKHAILOVICH. Maybe not better, but necessary. So now Katenka and Anatoly Dmitrich consider me a conservative and a reactionary, but I sympathize with all this. And when the old ways break down, though I shouldn't, I still sympathize. So now our young generation is growing. And Lyubochka'll either marry this one or another, but it won't be to the likes of us, but to a new, modern person. And Petrushka is also growing up understanding things differently. Well, I don't want to be an enemy of our own children. By the way, where's Petya? Could he be with his teacher?

MARYA VASILEVNA. They went to the lake, they wanted to fish for some kind of plants. I didn't understand. I'm even afraid they may have drowned. *Vraiment, je crains.*

IVAN MIKHAILOVICH. Fish for what plants?

KATERINA MATVEYEVNA. Aleksey Pavlych said that they wanted to conduct research on the structures of fibers in waterplants.

IVAN MIKHAILOVICH. Well, such are the times! Did I really have any idea of this as a boy, but now here's my boy who's already into natural science...and all that. Yes, that student has turned out real good. We should thank Anatoly Dmitrich, he recommended him. He's a good one, so calm...nice.....good, good. Hey, Sashka, my pipe! (*To* KATERINA MATVEYEVNA.) Old habit, you see! Please, Aleksandr Vasilich. (*Enter* SASHKA *with the pipe.*)

MARYA VASILEVNA (*suddenly angered*). Well, everyone is good in your eyes except your wife! So why doesn't he have any linen? Nannie gave him all the guest bedding. If someone comes, there'll be nothing to make up a bed with. What's this just coming in a coat, nothing else. I'll not give him my sheets. See how you judge things!

IVAN MIKHAILOVICH. Well, she's off. Enough, please, tell Nannie, she'll see to it. I'm happy for the man, that he's a sensible fellow.

MARYA VASILEVNA. So what if he's sensible? It's not my fault that he came with nothing and demands everything. He's now taken it into his head to drink milk. Besides, Dunyasha has been complaining. You have to keep an eye on him. What kind of teacher could he be if he has no linen.

IVAN MIKHAILOVICH. Well, she's at it again... You should thank God that He sent us such a man. And if he's poor and has no linen, then we have to give him some.

MARYA VASILEVNA. You never do understand me, it's all to the contrary. I'm saying that you're doing things wrong, but I feel sorry for him more than you do. I've felt sorry for him from the first time he sat down to eat! I sent him some nightshirts and even had them knit some socks for him. I may be stupid, but I understand that as our son's teacher, he's the number one person in the house. I don't begrudge him anything. I'm merely saying, put everything in order. Now how many times have I asked the carpenter to fix the leg on the table...

IVAN MIKHAILOVICH. Well, enough, my dear, stop, for Christ's sake!

SCENE 4

THE SAME *and the* STUDENT.

STUDENT (*enters with a slight bow*). May I have some tea. (*Sits down next to* KATERINA MATVEYEVNA.)

MARYA VASILEVNA. What would you like, Aleksey Pavlovich? Tea or coffee, with bread and butter, what would you like? (*Moves everything over to him.*)

STUDENT. Whatever. Well, make it tea.

IVAN MIKHAILOVICH. Where's Petrusha?

STUDENT. He'll make his entry. He's changing his trousers. He got soaked.

IVAN MIKHAILOVICH. What was it you were doing?

STUDENT. We wanted to study botany, but it went awry. So we indulged in fishing.

IVAN MIKHAILOVICH. But Katenka said you wanted to study something in the natural sciences...

STUDENT. We wanted to, but it went awry. There was no microscope on hand.

MARYA VASILEVNA. Do you want bread with it? Please eat.

STUDENT (*to* KATERINA MATVEYEVNA). What kind of soul-satisfying reading are you conducting? (*Takes the book from her.*) Oh, it's physiology—that's a good article, only too sketchy. You should have a look at Lewes.[2] And also "Transmutation of the Cell," I forgot by whom; it's not a bad little article.

MARYA VASILEVNA. What are cells? Is that what they're really called? Help yourself to some cream, they'll bring more. Katenka, do you also know what cells are?

KATERINA MATVEYEVNA. All organic matter exists as a result of the development of cells.

STUDENT (*to* KATERINA MATVEYEVNA). Why give explanations in vain? At least elementary knowledge is required for that.

IVAN MIKHAILOVICH. I have read about cells. Just tell me, Aleksey Pavlich, can they be seen in bread?

STUDENT. Were they not seen, they could not have been spoken about or studied. They're visible through a microscope.

IVAN MIKHAILOVICH. Does a microscope cost a lot?

STUDENT. You can acquire a lousy one cheap. Anatoly Dmitrievich has one; it costs 360 francs, but the one at the university is fifteen thousand.

IVAN MIKHAILOVICH. Yes, we have to buy one. (*Sits down beside his wife on one side of the table, while the* STUDENT *and* KATERINA MATVEYEVNA *are on the other side.* IVAN MIKHAILOVICH *smokes in silence.*)

KATERINA MATVEYEVNA (*quietly speaking to the* STUDENT). You have just missed another outrageous scene here, truly plantationesque.

STUDENT. Well, they can make fun of the likes of themselves. That's all they're really capable of... As for me, I must tell you, I'm bored here, I want to leave and get my degree.

KATERINA MATVEYEVNA. I take a different view. I find that the cruder the environment in which one must work, the greater is the energy one must expend. For, by virtue of what can these abnormal relations be changed, if not by virtue of the ideas and input that we will introduce into them? I recognize my influence on these people and use it to the utmost. Now you are charged with improving the as yet immature personality of Pyotr. For his part, he, too, introduces ideas into this numbing environment. And Anatoly Dmitrich also thinks along these lines.

STUDENT. Well, may God have mercy upon them! If you wade in muck, you'll get dirty. Let the Toothbusters[3] enjoy themselves in their way, and we in our own way. You can't protest every step of the way, then you only feel your indignation weaken. There are peasants who plow from four o'clock in the morning, but here they drink tea until noon. How's one to reconcile oneself to that?

KATERINA MATVEYEVNA. You are right, but, nevertheless, we have to make concessions. On the other hand, Venerovsky, who moves in the most backward circle at his job, basically does not concede a thing, but keeps on advancing ideas.

STUDENT. What's Venerovsky to me? I cannot respect a man who's in the Civil Service. These liberal excisemen!

KATERINA MATVEYEVNA. Excuse me, excuse me! You and I will never come to a complete understanding in this. Venerovsky is a remarkable person. Just look at his activities—schools, public lectures.

STUDENT. Very well, I can put the seal of silence on my lips.

KATERINA MATVEYEVNA. I find it funny to recall the conversation I had today about him with the old dames. How these people understand people of our cast! Just imagine, in their view he keeps coming here only in order to marry Lyubov Ivanovna, or rather, her dowry, as they explain it.

STUDENT. And why not, from that highly respected *seignior* all sorts of abominations could occur.

KATERINA MATVEYEVNA. Don't speak like that, Tverdynskoy, otherwise we will part company... Venerovsky marry! And to whom!

STUDENT. Okay, I'll explain myself to you. Lyubov Ivanovna is not a bad girl. There are some nice things about her character. Were she to fall into the hands of a wholesome, moral, and energetic man, she could be made into a respectable individual. Only she needs a young, honest mentor.

KATERINA MATVEYEVNA. But she is so underdeveloped!

STUDENT. So what, she would develop.

KATERINA MATVEYEVNA (*after a thoughtful pause*). Yes, perhaps I agree with you on this point. You are the very man who would be able to have a positive influence on her personality.

STUDENT. Were she not in this vile environment, it would be possible to make a respectable young lady out of her.

SCENE 5

Enter PETRUSHA, *a boy of about fifteen, in a school uniform.*

MARYA VASILEVNA. Well, here's our Petinka. What would you like, some tea, coffee?

PETRUSHA. Greetings, Mother. Nothing. I've had milk already. Mother, have them serve breakfast. Greetings, Father.

IVAN MIKHAILOVICH. What's this clowning, be natural, please.

PETRUSHA. You're wrong in thinking that I'm clowning. Greetings, Father is all I'm saying.

IVAN MIKHAILOVICH. Have you gone out of your mind? What's this new thing you've come up with! Greet us the way you used to greet us. Do you really think this is the educated way? Go and kiss your mother's hand.

PETRUSHA. Why should I?

IVAN MIKHAILOVICH (*sternly*). I'm telling you to.

PETRUSHA. What for? Will something really come of my touching the exterior portion of Mother's hand with the extremities of my lips?

IVAN MIKHAILOVICH. I'm telling you, kiss her hand.

PETRUSHA. That is contrary to my convictions.

IVAN MIKHAILOVICH. What?!

PETRUSHA. Aleksey Pavlovich and I talked about that, and it has become very clear to me that this is a stupid bias.

IVAN MIKHAILOVICH. Take care, Brother!

PETRUSHA. It's nothing, Father. You see, I won't change my view of you and Mother because of this. Whether I kiss your hands or not, I'll have as much respect for the both of you as you deserve.

IVAN MIKHAILOVICH. Now you listen to me. All this is fine, your new convictions and so forth, but one has to know limits, and the first rule from the beginning of time has been to respect your elders. Go kiss her hand. (*Begins to rise.*) Well!

STUDENT. It looks as though there'll be a major scandal here.

PETRUSHA (*becoming timid*). Of course, you can force me. But a man's free relations...

IVAN MIKHAILOVICH. Well! Well!

PETRUSHA (*kisses her hand, speaks quietly*). A man's dignity...

MARYA VASILEVNA. Now, Petya, just obey. What will you have, an omelette or pate? I'll see to it. Nannie, set the table for Petya's breakfast.

IVAN MIKHAILOVICH. Aleksey Pavlovich, h'm...h'm...although...you will forgive me, but...allow me to tell you that I asked you to study the sciences with my son, and not in any way to teach him how to treat his parents. We have our own, perhaps strange and old-fashioned customs. And I would ask you not to interfere in this.

STUDENT. H'm...huh...huh...well.

IVAN MIKHAILOVICH. Well and that's it. Your business is teaching about cells, and I ask you not to interfere in our son's treatment of us, and not to give him any ideas.

STUDENT. I find it rather strange listening to these reprimands. What do you want to say?

IVAN MIKHAILOVICH. This is what I want to say, that my son shouldn't speak such nonsense to me, that's all.

STUDENT. Well then, you can thrash him.

IVAN MIKHAILOVICH. Listen, don't make me lose my temper.

STUDENT (*becoming timid*). I understand very well... But, believe me, I don't presume to... However, you wanted me to educate your son. I, I...very much... After all, I cannot hide my views from him.

KATERINA MATVEYEVNA. It would be rather strange were Aleksey Pavlovich to pass over in silence or ignore, so to say, the deductions of science.

PETRUSHA. I can have my own convictions myself.

STUDENT. All the more so since life has its own rights, and prejudice does not hold up against intellectual and scientific criticism.

KATERINA MATVEYEVNA. There is no room for regressive views, especially given the enormous strides that have been made by the natural sciences.

IVAN MIKHAILOVICH. Well, fine, fine, Let's not speak about it. I'm going to ask my son to do what I want, and that's that. (*After a short pause, to the* STUDENT.) Have I offended you, Aleksey Pavlovich?

STUDENT. I value my dignity too highly to take offense. It's time for us to study. Pribyshev junior, let's march.

PETRUSHA. No, I want to eat. (*Enter* SASHKA *with a dish.*)

STUDENT. Well, let's stay, it won't hurt to have a bite. (*Moves closer to the table.*)

SCENE 6

LYUBOCHKA, *in a tucked-up dress and straw hat, runs in with a basket of mushrooms, followed by two* GIRLS.

LYUBOCHKA. Momma darling, you know I haven't come alone!

MARYA VASILEVNA. Who's with you?

IVAN MIKHAILOVICH. Who with?

LYUBOCHKA. Try and guess! It's Anatoly Dmitrievich. I'm walking with the girls, and here he comes riding and joins me. And we found two beautiful white mushrooms in the ditch, near the trees in the yard. Marvelous, what beauties! But Anatoly Dmitrievich doesn't see a thing, he only found one toadstool. Just look at these darlings! Katinka, take a look. Mashka, you have them, give them to me. (*She takes the basket from the* GIRLS *and gets the mushrooms.*) Sashka, just look at all these brown-cap mushrooms. And you said there were no mushrooms in the birch alley. Daddy, do you see them?

IVAN MIKHAILOVICH. But where's Anatoly Dmitrievich?

LYUBOCHKA. He's brushing off his trousers. He fell on his knees and got dirty. He's wearing white trousers. Daddy, what things we talked about, shocking! Well, I'll tell you later when we're alone.

IVAN MIKHAILOVICH. What is it? What?

LYUBOCHKA. Something very important, but I can't say anything now, it concerns me...

IVAN MIKHAILOVICH. But you're not really doing right walking around in the woods just like that, alone with a young man... Let's assume...but nevertheless.

LYUBOCHKA. Now that's an old-fashioned idea! Isn't that right, Katinka?

IVAN MIKHAILOVICH. What, you too! Well, come on over here, tell me, what were these important things you talked about?

LYUBOCHKA. I can't now. Wait a bit, you'll find out. But, Momma, just look at these darlings. (*Posing with her arms at her sides, she forms the shape of a mushroom.*) Just like our teacher, Karl Karlych, do you remember?—small, fat. Oh, how happy I am today! Sashka, tomorrow we'll get going ear..r..rly.

MARYA VASILEVNA. Well, do you want some tea, coffee with rolls?

LYUBOCHKA. You'll be surprised, Dad, at what we spoke about. And you would too, Katya, and you...and you'll be surprised, Aleksey Pavlovich. Give me some, what are you eating? (*Pulls the fork away from him and puts a piece in her mouth.* PYOTR *continues to eat eagerly.*)

KATERINA MATVEYEVNA (*to the* STUDENT). And that's an equal to Anatoly Dmitrievich? What immaturity!

STUDENT. Still judging by her figure and face she's respectable and not at all bad.

LYUBOCHKA. Momma, may I give them each a piece? (*Points to the* GIRLS *and gives them each a piece of roll and sugar.*) Come again tomorrow ear..r..ly.

MARYA VASILEVNA (*handing her a cup of tea*). Here, have some with cream.

LYUBOCHKA. I don't feel like eating, I took a piece of the heel from Maska, it was so good, marvelous! (*Sits down at the table and immediately speaks.*) Dad, I even forgot to kiss you. (*Kisses him.*) You're my white mushroom! What were you arguing about when I came in?

IVAN MIKHAILOVICH. Your brother here has taken it into his head that you don't have to kiss your father, but you have to say: Greetings, Father! Greetings, Mother!

PETRUSHA (*still chewing*). I took nothing into my head, I arrived at this conviction.

LYUBOCHKA. Ha, ha, ha! What nonsense! They always take new things into their heads.

IVAN MIKHAILOVICH. And is your new thing to stroll alone with young men?

LYUBOCHKA. Sh! Don't get on me! I'll purposely go with a young man. Aleksey Pavlovich, let's go together after mushrooms tomorrow.

STUDENT. Well, that could be arranged.

LYUBOCHKA. I'm afraid not, I won't be able to.

MARYA VASILEVNA (*to the* STUDENT). Wouldn't you like an omelette?

STUDENT. No, I wouldn't, I'm full. Well, Pribyshev junior, have you had your fill? Let's march. (*Exit the* STUDENT *and* PETRUSHA.)

SCENE 7

THE SAME and the FOREMAN.

IVAN MIKHAILOVICH. Hm....... What now?

FOREMAN. They've stopped mowin' in the gravel field.

IVAN MIKHAILOVICH. Why's that? What about the freed ones?

FOREMAN. Our peasants chased 'em away. A fight broke out between 'em. Matorin was beat up badly. He's at the office waitin'.

LYUBOCHKA. Oh, I forgot to tell you. He looks frightening, just like a bandit. I got so scared, Momma.

IVAN MIKHAILOVICH. Why the fight?

FOREMAN. The mowers were out, they just set up—here comes Dyomkin runnin' with his bunch of trash—they used to do the plowin' here—how dare yuh, he says, mow our master's lands! He hired us, they say. That's right, he says, you're real slick, reducin' our price. Now yuh're gonna mow an acre for a ruble in silver! He would've given us two, if he had no other way, or we might've got grazin' for the horses. And he began to fight. Now the men came runnin' from the field, and they beat 'im up badly.

LYUBOCHKA. His whole head is still bloody, he looks horrible.

IVAN MIKHAILOVICH. Where were you? That's your business, you know. What about the overseer?

FOREMAN. He went to the constable.

IVAN MIKHAILOVICH. Great, real great!

FOREMAN. What can I say, Ivan Mikhalych, there's nothin' yuh can do with these folks. Last night two more ropes were stolen. They almost swiped the iron-cased wheels, but luckily I saw 'em. How many times have I told 'em to lock things up—they don't listen. And it's me that has to answer for everythin'. I've, yuh know, done my best, I've not spared myself, yuh know. Just do me this favor, lemme go.

IVAN MIKHAILOVICH. Come on, my friend, easy!

FOREMAN. No, I can't, just do me this favor.

IVAN MIKHAILOVICH. You really must be joking! How can I possibly do this at the height of the season?

FOREMAN. That's up to you, Ivan Mikhalych, but I'm no longer yer servant. I did my best. It's only grief with these folks. Lemme go.

IVAN MIKHAILOVICH. Go and manage now! (*Paces nervously. Stops in front of the* FOREMAN.) You swine! Do you really think you can screw up and foul up, and then leave at the height of the season?

FOREMAN. That's how it is!

IVAN MIKHAILOVICH. Get out! I just don't want to dirty my hands. That's plain highway robbery. Who the hell knows what's going on! (*Paces.*)

MARYA VASILEVNA. It's just as I was saying, now all of them will leave.

LYUBOCHKA. Daddy, you should use freed workers. Anatoly Dmitrievich says that that's best.

IVAN MIKHAILOVICH. All of you can go to blazes! Talking nonsense, you don't know about what. I should put on blinders and run off! Everything's a mess, has fallen apart, they pilfer, they steal, nobody does any work! Squirts are teaching their elders. Everyone's gone crazy. That's progress for you!

KATERINA MATVEYEVNA. In my opinion the reasons for this are deeply rooted in our social structure.

IVAN MIKHAILOVICH. Leave me alone, for Christ's sake! (*To the* FOREMAN.) Well, are you going to stay? I'm asking you to stay. You know I can't just find someone else right away.

FOREMAN. There's no way I can. I already have another job.

IVAN MIKHAILOVICH (*angrily*). All right, so do you think you can get away with this? You bandit! All right. Off to the lockup with you!

FOREMAN. You won't dare, them days are gone.

IVAN MIKHAILOVICH. Me, not dare? (*Seizes him by the collar.*)

MARYA VASILEVNA (*jumping up*). *Jean!* Ivan Mikhailovich, what has got into you! Don't, for my sake!

IVAN MIKHAILOVICH. I'll take care of you in my own way. Let's go, you bastard! (*Takes him to the door. Exit* MARYA VASILEVNA *and* LYUBO-CHKA.)

SCENE 8

Enter VENEROVSKY.

VENEROVSKY. Here I am in the flesh—your hand!

IVAN MIKHAILOVICH. That's impossible! What's there to do?

VENEROVSKY. What's your problem? Has life got you down? Well, that's a good one. Ha, ha, ha!

IVAN MIKHAILOVICH. There's nothing I can do! Here's a man who's bene-fited from me, I freed him before the Manifesto, gave him land. He managed my estate and now, all of a sudden and for no reason...

VENEROVSKY. He doesn't want to remain in your service, ha ha! Well, that happens all the time. You'd like to beat him, torture and burn him over a slow fire, but you can't. What's there to do! That's the bad side of free labor.

IVAN MIKHAILOVICH. Well, the hell with him! (*To the* FOREMAN.) Get going, turn everything over to the overseer. I'll be coming. (*Exit* FORE-MAN.)

VENEROVSKY. By God, I admire you, Ivan Mikhalych. How you are over-coming yourself. That takes strength! Yes indeed, strength. And they call you a reactionary, ha, ha.

MARYA VASILEVNA. Would you like some tea, coffee with cream? Here are rolls and butter.

VENEROVSKY. *Merci.* Well, overall, how's the free labor? When I drove up, I saw: work's in full swing, ha, ha! How's it going?

IVAN MIKHAILOVICH. Ah, don't ask! It's going, but there are some prob-lems. How are you doing?

VENEROVSKY. We're okay, doing some work. All this government corruption is oppressing, stifling. We're trying to fight it.

IVAN MIKHAILOVICH. Oh yes, yes.

VENEROVSKY. And we're moving along, slowly but surely. Yesterday we opened a school for the children of goldsmiths. We procured premises and so forth, and managed to raise money for books from the merchants. It's going pretty well. Why don't you come sometime with Lyubov Ivanovna to see? It's interesting.

IVAN MIKHAILOVICH. Your efforts are praiseworthy. Well, when are you going to give your next lecture?

VENEROVSKY. I don't have time, I'm always busy. The factory owners cheat a lot. I caught one three days ago. He offered me a three-thousand-rouble bribe, ha, ha! Ridiculous people, not even worth getting offended over. What can you do, it's as if they're speaking Chinese, ha, ha, ha! Why don't you come one of these days with Lyubov Ivanovna to see the school? You know, you work, and work, you look around, and nevertheless you feel that this district circle is being improved at least somewhat. Although they hate me, ha, ha, who cares! As for me, I don't hate but despise them.

IVAN MIKHAILOVICH. What was it that happened at your club?

VENEROVSKY. We caught a crook there—the manager was about to swipe club money but we caught him in the act. But there are lots more swindlers, ha ha! That's why you're happy when you notice that the ideas of progress, a sense of honor and human feeling are slowly beginning to penetrate their thick skulls, at least to some degree. Say what you want, but even one single honest person can do a great deal. Just take me, why should I be modest, ha, ha!

IVAN MIKHAILOVICH. How can you blame them, what kind of education did they get?

VENEROVSKY. But I've come to you on a small personal matter. (*Takes him aside.*) You know, however much one may think about public affairs, occasionally one must think about oneself—selfish feelings nevertheless remain in every man. This happens to me rarely, but now there is this extraordinary case... I don't even know how to put it! Actually, I've grown so unaccustomed to looking after my own interests. (*Smirks.*) It's actually funny...

IVAN MIKHAILOVICH. What is it, could it be money that you need? I'm always ready, in keeping with my means...

VENEROVSKY. No! I know you don't like me, but what's there to do! After all, we have the power. You have to take us into account.

IVAN MIKHAILOVICH. Yes, I think I can finally guess...but this is a matter in which...

VENEROVSKY. Well, if you've guessed, then let me have your daughter, that's it! But please, just do it as simply as possible.

IVAN MIKHAILOVICH (*solemnly*). Your proposal, Anatoly Dmitrievich, pleases me. I've always had the highest opinion of you. And what you've just done confirms my good thoughts. You've acted like a truly honorable man. It's not without a purpose that you've been coming to my home; you've not compromised my girl. Besides, like a truly noble man, you didn't wish to embarrass the girl but first spoke to her father. That's a highly noble trait.

VENEROVSKY. Well, that's not quite the way we would look at this, ha ha. I've already spoken to Lyubov Ivanovna. She wants to, ha ha!

IVAN MIKHAILOVICH. Hm... Yes...you know... Well all right, I agree...

VENEROVSKY. I assume Marya Vasilevna will also... Ha, ha...all right. There's just one thing... You know, you think I'm strange, ha, ha! I'd find all the congratulations and gossiping unpleasant... I'd like to see less of the people whom I despise. Therefore, keep this in secret for the time being; all these ceremonies, you see, are foolish.

IVAN MIKHAILOVICH. Fi...fine, I understand. Now, son-in-law to be...

VENEROVSKY. Ivan Mikhailovich! I'm still Anatoly Dmitrievich and you're Ivan Mikhailovich, other than that, what's this son-in-law and father-in-law! There's no point to this, I find it unpleasant and, what's more, foolish.

IVAN MIKHAILOVICH. That's quite so, but... Well, I now feel I have to tell you about Lyubochka's means. We're not wealthy, but still...

VENEROVSKY. Now you're not doing me a good turn... What do I care about her means? Her means are her means. If she has some, so much the better. It seems to me that anyone who understands people even slightly can see my activities, and judge me by them. I'll tell you what I need. I have but one goal. This girl is a good person, she has good potential. I'm not in love with her. I don't recognize such foolishness.

She has potential, but she's not developed, indeed she's very underdeveloped. I want one thing: to raise her level to ours, and then I'll say: I have done another deed—and I wouldn't want anyone to interfere with me in this matter. I'm telling you this in advance. Perhaps it might seem strange to you but we're new people,[4] and what's strange and difficult for you is simple for us. So don't say anything to anyone before the first of August, and things will turn out fine. (*Shakes his hand.* IVAN MIKHAILOVICH *gives him a long and firm handshake.*)

IVAN MIKHAILOVICH. I understand it all, I understand. Let me embrace you.

VENEROVSKY. No, please don't. I find it unpleasant. Good-bye! (*Exit* VENEROVSKY.)

IVAN MIKHAILOVICH. A most noble man, indeed. Here's the new era! But still it's somewhat strange—I'm not used to it. But thank God, thank God!

ACT II

PART I

Dramatis personae
Ivan Mikhailovich Pribyshev
Katerina Matveyevna Dudkina
Anatoly Dmitrievich Venerovsky
Sergey Petrovich Bekleshov
    Venerovsky's university friend
Footman

SCENE 1

The set depicts an untidy bachelor's room in VENEROVSKY's *apartment.*

VENEROVSKY (*alone, holding his portrait in his hands*). Get married! It's frightening, it's stupid to tie oneself forever to an underdeveloped and socially corrupted woman. Why? In essence, you just want...nothing more... But you're taking absurd obligations upon yourself because of a bunch of riffraff. That's what's so disgusting. Let's suppose I understand the matter as not taking any obligation upon myself, but she doesn't understand it as such. She's incapable of this freedom of attitude. No. She's not really foolish, just underdeveloped. Now Dudkina is another matter; but then again she's plain, yes, unattractive. However, this one attracts me. What a strange feeling I had when I kissed her, and she returned my kiss. A pleasant feeling! Yes. I didn't expect it. Nevertheless (*looking at his portrait*) it was good... Very good. Very, very good. And before this I thought I wasn't good-looking. It's frightening to lose one's purity and strength in constant encounters with nonentities and trash—but pleasant. There's much that's pleasant. A secure life...besides she herself, as a woman...is not bad. I could retire. I could write... But most important—she's very pleasant. This is all magnificent. A magnificient woman!...... And, moreover, she kissed me with pleasure, even enormous enthusiasm. I experienced a feeling that I hardly could have expected. Yes indeed, I did not expect it. Why didn't I expect it? It's surprising how mistaken I was about myself. Indeed, to what degree I didn't understand myself. (*Looks in the mirror.*) Yes, a fine face, splendid looks. It's even very, very fine. Yes, that's what's called a handsome man; very attractive, a man of splendid looks. And the extent to which you don't know yourself! It's funny now to recall how nervous I was when I approached her. As though there was something to fear, ha, ha! Before this I thought that my looks were not very attractive, and I tried to console myself. Well, I thought to myself, I'm not as attractive as others, but then I'm intelligent because whom do I know more intelligent than me? Who else understands things as subtly, easily, and profoundly? Well, I thought to myself, I'm not good-looking and can't compete with those handsome guys who ride along the streets on trotters, but then again, I thought to myself, I have a formidable intellect, strength of character, pure liberal-mindedness, honesty... All this compensates me indirectly. That's how I consoled myself. I thought to myself: I can't get on in drawing rooms, I can't babble in French like the others, and I used to be envious of gentlemen of the salons. Well, I thought, but then again I'm educated better than anyone...and indeed, I don't know anyone with such a comprehensive and thorough education. Is there a discipline in which I would not feel myself capable of making discoveries—philology, history, and, of course, the natural sciences? I'm familiar with all this. As for talent... And I think to myself: that's how fate is, to some, like to me, it allots intelligence, talent, education, power, to others, banal gifts—good looks, grace, amiability. And then, how does it turn out? It turns out that nature did not allot but combined all this in one person. And all this is because in Petersburg I didn't have the chance to test my power over women...of this sort. But here it is. In the very best aristocratic circle and in the most banal, where they see only appearances. Because Lyuba is indeed incapable of understanding the essence of my merits... Two women have fallen *in love* with me. Yes, they've fallen in love. (*Smugly.*) Yes, I must be very unattractive and awkward... It's funny to remember how I didn't know myself! (*Looks at himself in the mirror.*) Yes, very nice... And if you combine it with my moral stature, which nevertheless is felt by them—no matter how inferior they are—it turns out that there are very few such people. Perhaps there aren't any at all. (*Frowns. Looks in the mirror.*) What a thoughtful, tranquil, astute expression! Yes, it's difficult to resist. I understand this. And along with this, if I only want to, I could at once lead that very same life which any of those hollow swells, aristocrats lead. Who's stopping me? I've worked enough for the good of society. I can relax, and relax not by myself, but with that fresh little flower that I, yes, I, will pluck. Why shouldn't I travel abroad, settle in Italy with a young wife, stay in the best hotel? Promenades.......... She in silk and velvet, fresh, pretty, on trotters, in a carriage; and at her side a remarkable and handsome man. Or in the evening, she in a low-cut dress, bare shoulders. Let 'em look from the pit. In Florence, in box seats, she and I, a man in a black English dress coat, simple, dignified, and with this brow and thoughtful, charming expression. Home in the evening, supper, and then... Yes, all this is civil, all this is captivating. And I thought that this is not meant for me. How you underestimate yourself. However, that's what a strong character means. You always underestimate your own worth, unlike all the trash who imagine themselves as God knows what. But it turns out that there isn't a man more fortunately endowed and at the same time less appreciative of his own merits. Yes... That's clear.

VENEROVSKY; *enter* BEKLESHOV, *a university friend of* VENEROVSKY
and functionary in community services.

BEKLESHOV. Well, pal, we had excellent sport today. Ha, ha! I've just
come from council chambers.

VENEROVSKY. It's commendable that you devote yourself to the labors of
life. What did God grant you now?

BEKLESHOV. We nailed three landowners, pal—a couple of gentlemen
and a lady—and indicted a bribe-taking functionary. All in one ses-
sion. It was fun, I must say!

VENEROVSKY. That's good. It serves them right, while I enjoy hearing of it
and you take pleasure in it.

BEKLESHOV. Indescribable pleasure, old pal! Of course, my entire life
hangs on this. It's my passion and specialization. Your brethren, the
idealists, just syllogize, while we, practioners, act. Why then am I taking an interest in your marriage? It's not at all because I'm your friend
and companion, or that I see that it's a question of your happiness.
Not at all. The only thing that I see in it is this mammal Pribyshev, who
intends to dupe you and who should be nailed, and I'll nail 'im. Well,
how are things? Are we going to the Pribyshevs today? After all,
today's the formal announcement. I'm ready and fully armed.

VENEROVSKY. What's to say, there's little good. Ha, ha, ha! Today's the
engagement. Quite a foolish business and it ought to be bypassed as
much as possible.

BEKLESHOV. That's nothing at all. What's the financial situation like? Was
it clarified?

VENEROVSKY. Now here comes your practical turn of mind!

BEKLESHOV. Could it be otherwise? That's the main point.

VENEROVSKY. On the very first day I explained myself to the esteemed
parent that her means are her means, and that he shouldn't give me
that dribble, yes, ha, ha! And the parent was significantly gladdened by
these views of mine—well, yes...

BEKLESHOV. Oh, these idealists! You know, you yourself gave him ammu-
nition. In keeping with his bovine nature, he'll assume that he doesn't

have to give your fiancée anything. But it's crazy to be responsible for supporting the woman without getting additional means. There's no need, it seems, to prove this.

VENEROVSKY. That's right. But I'll take measures nevertheless so as not to wind up the fool. My only goal is to tear this girl, a fine girl, out of the stultifying and demoralizing conditions in which she lives. And therefore it's obvious that this person shouldn't lose anything as a result of having chosen me, shouldn't be deprived of these, after all, simple comforts of life. I'll take measures to protect her interests.

BEKLESHOV. Just don't get trapped. Your brethren, idealists, are good at this. They make plans without discussing their feasibility. What measures will you take? Tell me, are you sure that her father will give her something specific, and will not want to keep a grip on you by forcing you to wait? People of this sort like to show off in front of the likes of us when you give them the chance.

VENEROVSKY. Well, though I'm not as practical as you, I have thought over this little matter and made my decision, yes, ha, ha... You see, this is how it is. The last time I saw Pribyshev he began to speak about money again in front of her; I said that I find it more convenient to speak about this matter face to face rather than parade it in public.

BEKLESHOV. That's the point, pal, you'll go about it delicately and they'll dupe you.

VENEROVSKY. Look, today's the day I've arranged for these negotiations. I intend to tell him that I want these matters clarified. That I guarantee.

BEKLESHOV. I'm telling you he'll dupe you. (*Thinks for a moment.*) Remember one thing: for them, for these kind of people, what's most important is ritual. This is where we can catch them. Remember one thing: don't go to church until you are holding in your hands the formal documents confirming her ownership of certain property.

VENEROVSKY. You're talking about this as though the entire matter for me is her means. I find this quite unpleasant. You're much too practical.

BEKLESHOV. Well, I've been saying all along—idealist! You're forgetting whom you're dealing with. They're as crooked as they come. They've been robbing their serfs and drinking the people's blood for five hundred years, and you want to idealize with them. You have an honorable goal—to save her—well, fine. But then, what are means to you! You know, that's childish, sophomoric!

VENEROVSKY. For me, pal, the other matter comes first.

BEKLESHOV. Fine, fine. Idealist! I'm saying, if I don't take you in hand, you'll get caught like a fish in a net. Well, speaking about that, we'll nail him. Well, tell me, how's this special someone?

VENEROVSKY. What's there to tell you, the little girl's appearance is very pretty, kind, gentle, and her character is not ruined entirely yet. She has potential for very good things. Over the past two weeks I've given her a lot to read, I've spoken with her a great deal. She's beginning to understand things as they are. For example, already she feels the vileness of her environment, wishes to tear herself away from it, and understands the worthlessness of her esteemed relatives. She has a very honest and good character. And she'll develop fully, I hope, once I've torn her away from this foul nest of all sorts of abomination, and, of course, broken all ties to her esteemed relatives. That's what you'll see today.

BEKLESHOV. Hm, hm. That's fine. Well, what kind of person is the niece?

VENEROVSKY. You see, the niece is an emancipated girl, a sensible and developed thing, but unattractive in appearance.

BEKLESHOV. Say what you want, but women aren't given both good looks and intellectual development. Those foolish, rosy-ish ones are more pleasant all the same.

VENEROVSKY. Ha, ha! Yes, of course. So this person is most inconvenient for me. You see, formerly there were some relations between me and that girl... She was the only thinking being in the whole family, and I unwittingly became close with her. Well, now it seems this person is making claims. Well, it's foolish, and perhaps it'll be even worse when she learns of my marriage.

BEKLESHOV. That's nasty.

VENEROVSKY (*proudly*). No, my esteemed Sergey Petrovich, no one can reproach me. I acted the way any honorable man who understands a woman's freedom should act. I told her then that I'm not assuming any obligations, that I'm involving myself in these relations only temporarily.

BEKLESHOV. Ha, ha, ha! You know I see what bothers you: you're thinking, didn't I act badly with regard to her? That's idealism indeed! Just think whom you're dealing with. Just remember what these people consider bad and good. You know, all moral concepts are distorted in the environment in which they live. If you take these people into consideration, you'll always be made the fool. The first rule is, what's dishonorable for us is honorable for them, and vice versa. Do take this into account. But, let's assume, you found pleasure with her—it's any port in a storm—so what follows from this?

VENEROVSKY. That's right, but this girl hangs on, thinks she's got a claim, and could hurt me. I'd like to remove her in general.

BEKLESHOV. That's understandable. Not only will I remove this influence, I'll couple these two personalities[5] so that you won't be able to uncouple them—just wait.

SCENE 3

THE SAME. *Enter, in dirty clothes, the* WATCHMAN, *an old man serving in the place of a footman, and then* KATERINA MATVEYEVNA *and* IVAN MIKHAILOVICH.

WATCHMAN. Anatoly Dmitrich, this young lady's asking for you again, and also a gentleman.

VENEROVSKY. What young lady?

WATCHMAN. Oh, the one who was here before, with short hair.

VENEROVSKY. That's Pribyshev with his niece. Let them in. (*Exit* WATCHMAN.)

BEKLESHOV. Now the game comes to the hunter. I'll nail them both. (*Enter* IVAN MIKHAILOVICH *and* KATERINA MATVEYEVNA.)

IVAN MIKHAILOVICH. Well, Katenka and I were at your school. Lyubochka wanted to go also but was afraid—she caught a cold yesterday. So, we've dropped in on you. I can tell you, Anatoly Dmitrievich, those children are real charmers, they're really something! Yes, its actually marvelous, marvelous!

VENEROVSKY. It's good that you've dropped in. Let me introduce you:

Bekleshov, my friend—an intelligent and fine gentleman. Katerina Matveyevna, meet my friend.

KATERINA MATVEYEVNA (*firmly grips* BEKLESHOV'*s hand so that he grimaces in pain; to* BEKLESHOV). And do you acknowledge the bonds of fellowship? I do not. It's just another fallacy. I assume that you entered into friendly relations not by virtue of fellowship, but by virtue of a unity of ideas. I have always been struck by the phenomenon that among men the bonds of fellowship are firm, whereas among women this phenomenon...is not reproduced, so to speak. Is the reason for this not rooted in the lower degree of education given to a woman? Isn't that so?

BEKLESHOV. Of course, the bond is strengthened by a unity of ideas, and not by...

KATERINA MATVEYEVNA. Excuse me, excuse me. I assume you are close with Anatoly Dmitrievich primarily not by virtue of your friendship, but by virtue of sharing the same convictions.

BEKLESHOV. Of course, we share the same convictions. Were you at the school?

KATERINA MATVEYEVNA. Yes. Tell me, what do you think: it occurred to me, could the development of introspection in boys be harmful? You will agree, after all one is dealing with far too integrated personalities...

BEKLESHOV. That is—I don't know how you are looking at this. Introspection is only an indication of development. (*They continue to speak and move aside.*)

IVAN MIKHAILOVICH (*to* VENEROVSKY). I've wanted to see that school for a long time—it's so interesting! Besides, I think it's now necessary for us to talk matters over, you remember, about Lyubochka's means. Look, I've brought this along. (*Points to his briefcase.*) It'll be more convenient for us here. We'll discuss it, and then I'll bring you to our place. Well, we can tell Katenka, since today everyone will know. She won't stand in the way but, quite the contrary, she'll give advice. Though she has some peculiarities, she's an intelligent person. Katenka!

VENEROVSKY. It's awkward now, you know, that gentleman...

IVAN MIKHAILOVICH. Well, it can wait. Only today I won't let you get away. You do have to know. (BEKLESHOV *and* KATERINA MATVEYEVNA *approach.*) Well, Anatoly Dmitrievich, I'm so thankful to you for allowing me to visit the school. Those kiddies are charmers, I can hardly get over it. They're so cheerful, inquisitive, what progress they're making, and it's so...something like... One has to give you credit, it's wonderfully done! It's marvelous. Now that's a good thing...marvelous, marvelous.

VENEROVSKY. Yes, we're working at it gradually. Though there's resistance, we're breaking it down.

IVAN MIKHAILOVICH (*to* BEKLESHOV). I find that there's no progress for our people without real education, I mean moral education.

BEKLESHOV. Yes, depending on how one understands moral education, it's useful, of course.

KATERINA MATVEYEVNA. Excuse me, excuse me! Anatoly Dmitrievich, why haven't you introduced the phonetic method? It is more accessible and rational, much more rational.

VENEROVSKY. Well, not everything is done rationally. I preferred Zolotov's[6] simplified method.

KATERINA MATVEYEVNA. Besides, I would also like to make a direct comment. Bekleshov and I were just speaking. I assume that it is irrational to develop introspection in inferior personalities.

IVAN MIKHAILOVICH. Excuse me, I just have to drop by the office, and then let's go and talk things over.

VENEROVSKY (*to* KATERINA MATVEYEVNA). Now we'll make some judgments, ha, ha, ha! (*To* IVAN MIKHAILOVICH.) Go ahead, you know Bekleshov will also be coming with us. There is room for him in your coach, isn't there?

IVAN MIKHAILOVICH. Lots of room, lots. (*To* BEKLESHOV.) I'm very happy, very. We'll have a nice day today. For us a friend of Anatoly Dmitrievich is a welcome guest. (*They speak quietly.*)

KATERINA MATVEYEVNA (*to* VENEROVSKY). If I remain here, I will participate in teaching at this school. I will prove to you in practice that introspection is harmful.

VENEROVSKY. Well, that's possible.

IVAN MIKHAILOVICH (*exiting*). So long then, I'll be ready in five minutes.

VENEROVSKY (*to* IVAN MIKHAILOVICH). Well, we'll see you, we'll see you. (*To* KATERINA MATVEYEVNA.) Why are you so against the development of introspection in children? I assume that what is good for us will be good for everyone.

KATERINA MATVEYEVNA (*to* VENEROVSKY). No, excuse me, excuse me. So many ideas have come to me as a result of my visit to this school! One question: What do you want to make out of these personalities? Do you acknowledge the development of each individual for the obvious good, or could the development of an individual without social initiative harm these individuals by virtue of the existing abnormal order?

VENEROVSKY. I acknowledge that development is always for the good in whatever forms it might assume, but...

KATERINA MATVEYEVNA. Yes, but add, on the path of progress.

VENEROVSKY. That goes without saying. But one does have to take into consideration the impediments of the surrounding environment.

KATERINA MATVEYEVNA. That's right, but say whatever you like, I told you already that instinctively I feel that this whole stifling situation and stagnant atmosphere which we breathe are beyond your power.

VENEROVSKY (*wants to say something to his friend*). You...

KATERINA MATVEYEVNA. No, excuse me, excuse me, let me finish. You have dedicated yourself to the idea of bringing light into this stagnation, but the environment will crush you, you need a broader arena. (*To* BEKLESHOV.) Isn't that so?

BEKLESHOV (*to* VENEROVSKY *quietly*). Well, pal—some damsel! Just try to get your point across.

KATERINA MATVEYEVNA (*after thinking a moment*). Yes. That visit has spawned such a mass of ideas. I have begun to respect you even more. (*Shakes* VENEROVSKY*'s hand and says to him quietly.*) Today is the day I set for you; I will explain myself today. I wish to speak with you alone. (*To* BEKLESHOV *loudly.*) Bekleshov, I am above social biases, I have personal business with Venerovsky, and therefore I ask you to leave. Are you above them?...

BEKLESHOV. Of course. I'll wait in that room. (*To* VENEROVSKY *exiting.*) So much the better. Yes, I can say she's developed, but unpleasant. (*Exits.*)

SCENE 4

THE SAME *without* BEKLESHOV. KATERINA MATVEYEVNA *is silent,* VENEROVSKY *smirks and is also silent.*

KATERINA MATVEYEVNA (*feeling confused*). Yes, today is that day...and, so to say...yes, the mental process is completed...but you are an honorable person... Woman has emerged already from beneath a social oppression in which she was stifled... She has the same rights as a man, and I...yes, I have to tell you honestly and directly...I have acquired a profound knowledge of myself...yes, I... But do say something!...

VENEROVSKY. I'll listen. It seems the conversation should be very interesting.

KATERINA MATVEYEVNA. Yes, but so to say...yes, wait a moment...

VENEROVSKY. I'll wait. You promised to communicate your feelings to me, but something is making you hesitate. You're an emancipated woman—get a grip on yourself. Clarity of expression and words is necessary for the clarity of relations. And for me definiteness in our relations is very desirable. I'll speak directly and you do the same without being embarrassed by antiquated views on the relations between a man and a woman. Don't hesitiate—it's old Adam, as the mystics of blessed memory used to say, confusing you... Well...

KATERINA MATVEYEVNA (*decisively*). Yes, that is so, it is old Adam. I am above this. (*Extends her hand.*) Venerovsky! I have plumbed the depths of my consciousness and have become convinced that we should unite! Yes... In which ways this union will take place—I leave to you. Should you find it necessary, in view of the throng and underdeveloped relatives, both mine and yours, to have a marriage ceremony performed—I, though it is highly contrary to my convictions, agree in advance and am making this concession. But I wish for one thing. This environment, as I have said already, is stifling you and oppressing me. We must leave here. We must settle in Petersburg, where we shall find greater empathy for our convictions, and there we must begin a new life, on new principles and bases. As for the question of possessing me, that has been decided already between us.

VENEROVSKY. Now that's honest and clear. I can at least express myself just as categorically, and I'll try to do so.

KATERINA MATVEYEVNA. Excuse me, excuse me, I have not said everything. The life that awaits us will have significance not only for us, but also for society as a whole. We shall be the prototype of new relations between a man and a woman, we shall be the realization of an idea of an era, we shall...

VENEROVSKY. Allow me also to say a word or two!

KATERINA MATVEYEVNA. Venerovsky! I respect you—you know me. I am a woman who is emancipated and of equal rights with a man. I am proud of the fact that I first said: I want to unite with you, and I expect an honest, conscientious answer. It is all very simple. (*Brushes her hair back and paces nervously.*)

VENEROVSKY. So you see, a simple and honest attitude toward life is more convenient and expedient. You say that you wish to unite with me. That's very clear: at least one knows what to answer. Your very choice and the way you expressed it all testifies to the high degree of development you have attained. I do not know any other young lady who would be able to act so conscientiously. I'll give a direct answer—this union is inconvenient for me and, therefore, I cannot partake in it. As concerns our former relations, then precisely that moral feeling for truth which you so strongly possess must be a guarantee of your modesty in this regard.

KATERINA MATVEYEVNA. Excuse me, excuse me... You are refusing me? (*Stops and brushes her hair back.*)

VENEROVSKY. Katerina Matveyevna, there isn't a modern man who would not consider your proposal a reward for his efforts, but I've made another choice and, therefore...

KATERINA MATVEYEVNA. Ah! Good, very good... Excuse me, I respect you. (*Paces nervously.*)

SCENE 5

THE SAME *and* IVAN MIKHAILOVICH.

KATERINA MATVEYEVNA. Ah, Ivan Mikhailovich! We had a talk, the situation has been clarified. Yes, I'm very happy about this definiteness.

Yes, we clarified everything.

IVAN MIKHAILOVICH. Was there really something unclear between you?

VENEROVSKY. More abstract questions.

KATERINA MATVEYEVNA. Excuse me, not entirely abstract... Well, anyway I'm very happy, let's go home...

IVAN MIKHAILOVICH. No, I'm sorry. I promised to talk matters over with Anatoly Dmitrievich today. I came here purposely and I've even brought the papers... Now, Katenka, you can be told. Congratulate me and Anatoly Dmitrievich. He proposed to Lyuba, which is flattering for us, and'll marry on the first of August.

KATERINA MATVEYEVNA (*to* VENEROVSKY). There are three kinds of love: love of Astarte,[7] love of Aphrodite, and love of equal rights... Venerovsky, you have not risen above love of Astarte. I thought more highly of you...but I still respect you. Ivan Mikhailovich, will you be long?

IVAN MIKHAILOVICH. No, about a quarter of an hour, just wait.

KATERINA MATVEYEVNA. Venerovsky, give me the latest *Polar Star*[8]—I'll browse through it.

VENEROVSKY (*gives her the journal*). Take a look at this article. He really handles this well... Wouldn't you like to move to that room so that we won't disturb you?

KATERINA MATVEYEVNA. No.

VENEROVSKY. It really would be better for you.

KATERINA MATVEYEVNA. No.

VENEROVSKY (*aside*). Again it's impossible to talk!

KATERINA MATVEYEVNA (*sits down at the table on the side, leans on her elbows and begins to read, glancing at* VENEROVSKY *from time to time and shaking her head doubtfully.* IVAN MIKHAILOVICH *sits down at the table, opens his briefcase, and rummages in the papers.* VENEROVSKY *sits down opposite him*).

IVAN MIKHAILOVICH. Well now, my dear, good Anatoly Dmitrievich...

VENEROVSKY. What is it? Go on.

IVAN MIKHAILOVICH. You were so noble the first time I began to speak about Lyubochka's means that you shied away from this conversation; I appreciate this very much, believe me. But you'll agree that for me, as a father, it's pleasant, so to say, to give an accounting of my management of my daughter's means, to give an accounting to her future husband...

VENEROVSKY. Well, I'm listening. Go on.

IVAN MIKHAILOVICH. I'll be frank. Perhaps another would be ashamed that people might think that he's money hungry, but obviously you, Anatoly Dmitrievich, need not be concerned in this regard. Surely no one would say that you married for money.

VENEROVSKY (*glances at* KATERINA MATVEYEVNA). Of course that's so. But all this doesn't bring us down to business.

IVAN MIKHAILOVICH (*rummaging in his papers, takes one*). You see, my assets are modest and will go to my son. Lyubochka will get her mother's assets. Her mother wishes to keep a small part for herself—we decided that the remainder will go to you...

KATERINA MATVEYEVNA (*stands up, brushes her hair back*). Excuse me, excuse me, Anatoly Dmitrievich, the respect that I had for your person is beginning to vacillate in the depths of my consciousness. Two weeks ago you expressed the view that you do not respect Lyubochka. That was in the order of things.

IVAN MIKHAILOVICH. Katenka, don't interfere—what are you dragging in!

KATERINA MATVEYEVNA. Excuse me, excuse me! Venerovsky, you expressed the view to me that you do not respect her as a woman, and now you are getting married. That is inconsistent.

VENEROVSKY. I don't understand why you're saying this.

KATERINA MATVEYEVNA. Excuse me, I said: you have acted inconsistently. That is all I said. Now you and Ivan Mikhailovich are discussing the financial affairs of your fiancée—it seems that is the word, isn't it? In this fact I see a base trafficking of a human being and, therefore, I ask you not to insult me, not to insult each other, and not to insult the dignity of a human being by continuing this conversation. I have had my say.

IVAN MIKHAILOVICH. All the same, Katenka, it's becoming tiring and foolish.

VENEROVSKY (*quietly to* IVAN MIKHAILOVICH). It's very strange, that's all I can say. This is a really tiring conversation, and if you wish to say something, say it to Bekleshov, actually I don't have time, and I'll mention it to him.

IVAN MIKHAILOVICH. So, Anatoly Dmitrievich, let's go to my place. Call him. Let's go!

KATERINA MATVEYEVNA. I will not permit this humiliation.

IVAN MIKHAILOVICH. Actually it is tiring, let's go.

VENEROVSKY. I'll follow you. (IVAN MIKHAILOVICH *and* KATERINA MATVEYEVNA *exit.*)

SCENE 6

BEKLESHOV (*comes out of the other room*). Well, pal, I can tell you that's an intense damsel. She has to be removed, absolutely removed.

VENEROVSKY. But how?

BEKLESHOV. I'm afraid of one thing, that this entire scene was staged and the zealous damsel Dudkina was prompted by this Toothbuster.

VENEROVSKY. No, the damsel acted in the simplicity of her foolish heart.

BEKLESHOV. I'm telling you that there isn't an abomination of which these folks aren't capable. But the point is that you are charging me with negotiating means with her father—tell him this on the way—and that he won't get away from me. As concerns the damsel, I know one thing: she is consumed by the need to love. We have to sic some guy on her, only then will she leave you alone. Let's go. I'll nail the both of them.

VENEROVSKY. A practical man,[9] yes. Ha, ha!

PART 2

Dramatis personae
Ivan Mikhailovich
Marya Vasilevna
Lyubov Ivanovna
Katerina Matveyevna
Pyotr Ivanovich
Tverdynskoy
Venerovsky
Bekleshov
Nannie
First gentleman guest
Second gentleman guest
Lady guest

The set depicts a country garden on the Pribyshevs' estate.

SCENE 1

MARYA VASILEVNA *and* NANNIE.

NANNIE. You see it turned out like I thought, Marya Vasilevna, ma'am, everything, just as I said. I said fiancé—and he's a fiancé. And no matter how many times I laid out the cards, the king of diamonds and the wedding card always turned up. That's how the cards fell.

MARYA VASILEVNA. Yes, Nannie, it's not easy to part with a daughter. When Ivan Mikhailovich told me today, it was as if something struck me right here. (*Points to the back of her head.*) My head still hurts. I've taken a walk but I don't feel any better. What with the dowry, the wedding, all this is so worrisome!

NANNIE. What's there for you to worry about? Everything's ready, it's all here.

MARYA VASILEVNA. There is one thing, the fiancé doesn't like guests, what's there to do? After all, I have to invite relatives. At least for today I've asked them all to come to dinner, Semyon Petrovich, Marya Petrovna...

NANNIE. Yuh're right, ma'am. Otherwise it's as if you're givin' your daughter away in secret. We didn't begin this, and it's not for us to end it. A wedding's serious business. Not to worry, your relatives are as good as his. He's stickin' his nose up in the air too much! What is he, some sort of prince? He's nothin' special.

MARYA VASILEVNA. You're always finding faults with him, Nannie, that's not good. Don't you forget, he'll be Lyubochka's husband. There's just a week left. And Lyubochka is so in love, so in love! I'm even surprised. Little Lyuba, little Lyuba, and before you turn around, in a year, she'll have a little Lyuba herself. And how did all this happen? No, Nannie, don't you speak badly about him. No doubt he's a very important man—that's what everyone says. He knows everything, has been everywhere, he's a writer. And whom don't they speak badly about?

NANNIE. In front of Lyubochka, ma'am, in front of Lyubov Ivanovna, I won't say a thing, but who's to tell you except for me? It's not good, this arrogance is out of place. What are you, some petty gentry? Why's he so conceited with your relatives? He's been abroad, so what—nowadays, ma'am, there isn't a lousy landed lady that's not been abroad. I've been abroad, I'm really somethin'! Everyone's goin' now, it's not like in the old days. Or, I'm a writer! So what's so amazin', a real wonder—take our Katerina Matveyevna! You know, we saw this already in her as a little one—she was so dumb, and as for tact and pleasantness, none at all, and even she was sayin' the other day that she got some things printed. Or take the younger boy of Father Deacon—he was kicked out of the seminary but he also gets things printed. That's nothin' to be surprised at now. Besides, he's got no wealth, no family. They say his father is such a drunkard that his son don't let him come to him. No manners... Something's not right. He can't even make a proper entry. He wants to do everythin' in a new way, a peculiar way. But there's nothin' at all. Even his jokes are somehow out of place.

MARYA VASILEVNA. Ah, Nannie, better be quiet! Such is our fate.

NANNIE. Yuh're right. Words won't help. Only one thing—I'll kiss your hands and feet, just listen to your mean and nasty Nannie Marya, just listen to my advice. I beg you for God's sake! Don't give him none of the money or the estate yet. All this, yuh know, is yours and no one can order yuh around. Give it all: the dowry, clothes, linen, diamonds, give it all in the proper way, but wait with givin' the money. After all, yuh don't know about him. Wait and see what comes of him. It's never too late to give. I know, yuh see, yuh'll leave nothin' for yuhself.

MARYA VASILEVNA. What foolish ideas you have, Nannie. Well, how's that possible?

NANNIE. For once do listen to a fool, yuh'll be thankful. I beg yuh for God's sake! There's no harm in it, yuh know. Give it about two months, a half a year, and if he respects his mother-in-law and is good to her, then yuh can give.

MARYA VASILEVNA. Ah, what a fool you are!

NANNIE. Would it really be better if he'll grab the dough and won't show yuh respect, and make her life miserable? The things he says about yuh now! To him yuh're worth no more than this stockin'. For once in your life listen to Mashka the fool, but if yuh don't listen, yuh'll cry. Though your elbow is near, yuh can't bite it.[10]

MARYA VASILEVNA. How foolish you are, Nannie. I'll speak to Ivan Mikhailovich. I'll speak to him without fail; here he comes.

SCENE 2

THE SAME, *enter* LYUBOCHKA *and the* STUDENT.

STUDENT. This was not an unsatisfactory excursion that you and I have taken.

LYUBOCHKA. Momma! How come they're not here! I went to meet them. In vain. Aleksey Pavlovich went all the way with me and was lying all the time.

STUDENT. We were making jokes about bucolic trysts. And the conversation proceeded in a not unpleasant manner.

LYUBOCHKA. Why are you showing off? I'm tired of you, speak more simply.

STUDENT. If my manner of expression seems unamiable to you, let's go to the swings, Lyubov Ivanovna. I'll perform a swinging motion.

MARYA VASILEVNA. Aleksey Pavlovich, wouldn't you like to have breakfast?

STUDENT. I can use some nourishment—that's fine. Lyubov Ivanovna, let's go, really, otherwise it'll be boring.

LYUBOCHKA. Well then be bored alone, I have things to do.

STUDENT. So that's how it is. Are these important exercises?

LYUBOCHKA. I have to read an article, the one Anatoly Dmitrievich gave me.

STUDENT. In vain!

LYUBOCHKA. Why are you pestering me—really, I'm tired of you.

NANNIE. All this is somehow wrong.

STUDENT. And I'm tired of you. But I respect your sex.

LYUBOCHKA. What treatment!

MARYA VASILEVNA. Aleksey Pavlovich, you do have to treat Lyuba differently now.

STUDENT. I learned this treatment from a very wise little book by the author Belov, published in '63, and printed by Serkin under the title: *The Treatment of Persons of the Fair Sex, or The Art of Being Attractive to Them.*

LYUBOCHKA. Momma, send him away; why does he pester me! It's time for Petrusha's lessons. Petrusha!

PETRUSHA (*shouts through the window*). What?

LYUBOCHKA. Call Aleksey Pavlovich, it's time for your lessons. Go, I'm really bored. I haven't been able to get rid of you since morning.

STUDENT (*insulted*). You have suddenly changed your manner of treating me, and I do not know on what bases.

LYUBOCHKA. There are no bases. Go away, that's all.

STUDENT. You were much more sociable before.

NANNIE. Sir, if I was her mother, yuh'd not speak with my daughter that way in front of me. I'd have your hide!

MARYA VASILEVNA. What's the matter with you, Nannie? Have you gone crazy? Enough. (*To the* STUDENT.) Really, Aleksey Pavlovich, why are you pestering her? Go to Petrusha, I'll send you breakfast. I have to speak with Lyuba.

STUDENT (*aside*). This mammalian subject is being possessed by anger. Well, breakfast won't harm me, have it sent. (*Exit.*)

PETRUSHA (*his voice*). Mother, send some sturgeon and wine.

MARYA VASILEVNA. Fine.

SCENE 3

NANNIE, MARYA VASILEVNA, *and* LYUBOCHKA.

LYUBOCHKA. Momma, what am I to do? Wherever I go, he's always behind me, and pesters me...like a gadfly...can't you tell him not to, really...I am quite different now.

MARYA VASILEVNA. Now then, your fiancé is coming today and everyone will be informed.

NANNIE. Well, missy of mine, yuh shouldn't have fooled around with 'im to begin with. Just give a little man like that this much (*shows her little finger*)—he'll take the whole hand. Yuh shouldn't have flirted. Yuh're always gettin' too friendly with strangers. That's what your flirtin' came to.

LYUBOCHKA. But I didn't flirt at all, Nannie. We just used to play together with Petrusha...and he's so repulsive! I don't say a word to him now, I study all the time, I read the books Anatoly Dmitrievich brought me, but he doesn't leave me alone.

NANNIE. Yuh got to be stricter. What's this with your being so nice! I wouldn't, if I had my way, I wouldn't let that trash into the house. Just wait—I'll give 'im an ear full. I'm the only one he's afraid of, yuh know, in this whole house. Let 'im...

LYUBOCHKA. Momma, Katenka still doesn't know that I'm engaged, does she?

MARYA VASILEVNA. No, sweetheart, only your father and Nannie know, no one else. That's how you wanted it. Everyone will be informed today.

LYUBOCHKA. Why aren't they back? Really, it's terrible. Momma, isn't he good-looking? Isn't that right, Nannie?

MARYA VASILEVNA. Yes, an important person.

LYUBOCHKA. And how clever! If only you could hear how he explains things to me. Katenka will really be angry! Well, it serves her right.

She's always saying that I'm underdeveloped. So now I'll develop. He says that I've developed a lot in two weeks. You know, Nannie, she's in love with him. She doesn't say so, but I know she is. Here they come, here they come! Momma, you won't cry now will you? Nannie, don't cry, please. He doesn't like that, and it is silly. That's all old-fashioned but we'll do things in a new way. You can't even begin to understand how, Nannie. I'm so happy! He's so clever, isn't he?

MARYA VASILEVNA. May God grant that all goes well. May God grant that all goes well!

NANNIE. There's nothin' bad.

LYUBOCHKA. What do you mean bad? He's perfect, isn't he?

SCENE 4

THE SAME; *enter* IVAN MIKHAILOVICH, VENEROVSKY, BEKLESHOV, KATERINA MATVEYEVNA, TVERDYNSKOY.

IVAN MIKHAILOVICH (*introducing* BEKLESHOV). This is Pyotr Sergeyevich Bekleshov, a friend of Anatoly Dmitrievich.

MARYA VASILEVNA. Welcome, I'm very pleased. (*To* VENEROVSKY.) How are you, Anatoly Dmitrievich? *Comment va votre santé?* (MARYA VASILEVNA *and* IVAN MIKHAILOVICH *go into the house.*)

KATERINA MATVEYEVNA. Where are you, Aleksey Pavlych? I have something to say to you.

STUDENT (*comes out of the house*). Pyotr Ivanych and I were eating.

BEKLESHOV (*to* KATERINA MATVEYEVNA). Please introduce me to the student.

KATERINA MATVEYEVNA. I understand, he is the one lively personality.

BEKLESHOV. I'm very, very pleased. (*Shakes his hand.*) Let's take a stroll, all right? (*The two exit.*)

LYUBOCHKA (*to* VENEROVSKY). What took you so long? I was so bored. I read both your articles, and I understood them.

VENEROVSKY. That's good. And I've been turning something over in my mind concerning you.

LYUBOCHKA. What were you thinking? Do I know?

VENEROVSKY. I don't think so, Lyubov Ivanovna. I was thinking today, and even put some of it down on paper. (*Gives her an article.*)

LYUBOCHKA. No, please, speak to me. I like that.

VENEROVSKY. Well, you see: I was thinking about our last conversation. I was thinking about woman; one of the principal missions of our age is the liberation of woman from the barbaric servitude in which she is suppressed.

LYUBOCHKA. Yes, why can't a woman get married a second time? I often thought about this. What if I just become tired of one husband and completely stop loving him...

VENEROVSKY. Yes, this is how the great doctrine on the emancipation of women is compromised on the lips of the throng. It isn't about that, not at all about that. A woman's freedom is about equal rights with man, and not being eternally at the beck and call of a father and then a husband. Woman must stand firmly on her own feet in society and be able to look that society straight in the eye.

LYUBOCHKA. Why is Katya always saying that I'm underdeveloped? I understand all the new ideas, I really do!

VENEROVSKY. Yes, it's difficult to explain my thought to you. But I'll try to be more concrete.

LYUBOCHKA. What did you say? Concrete? I also know—the gnosiological method. I also know efics... Well, say what you wanted to.

VENEROVSKY. Yes, I want to give you an example of what real freedom of woman is. Were I one of those backward gentlemen, who reign in our society, or superficial liberals, I would assume that by marrying you I acquire the right to you. You would be dependent on me, I would be dependent on you. We would not be able to make a move without insulting each other. For example: I get sick, you detest the sight of a sick person, but you have to be here; or your or my gallbladder doesn't empty its contents into the stomach, but we must be together and suffer and argue. Or, I want to use my money to buy books, but you, let's assume, want to buy...

LYUBOCHKA. Well, buy a sewing machine or appliances of some sort. I would just buy such things, but I really wouldn't buy a black velvet dress, though I wanted one very much. Heavy material becomes me. Well, what was it you were saying? I do like to listen to you.

VENEROVSKY. Yes, you see, the main thing in a marriage is the freedom and independence of both parties.

LYUBOCHKA. Oh, I understand this. Well, how would it be for me to know that you will order me around! I'm already tired of my governesses. We had Sarah Karlovna—you didn't know her. Oh, what a bore! I wouldn't marry you for anything if I knew that you would order me around. And I'm happy because we'll not be exactly strangers but equals... Anetochka Zaitsova, you saw her at our place, she's my friend, but she's really very underdeveloped, reads romances all the time. She's the one that says you only get married when you're in love. Is it possible to fall in love when you want to? And it's even worse to pretend. But when you're equals, it's very easy. They're just dreamers. How can you fall in love just like that, on command!

VENEROVSKY. Yes, Lyubov Ivanovna, for such girls like your girlfriend love is just a word. But we'll arrange our life so that I won't hinder your freedom, and you won't mine. If we wish we can marry, and if we get bored, we can divorce without hindering one another. Then our life doesn't have to be clouded by any prejudices. If you or I were suddenly to find it difficult to live together, we must have the right to divorce without blame, without bile. All this is new but simple.

LYUBOCHKA. That's fine! Wonderful! I understand all this. Did you really think me a fool? Katenka kept on saying so. I thought so myself. And now I see that I'm smart. I understand everything so quickly. When you just start speaking, I already know what you'll say. Really!

VENEROVSKY. The truth is simple, that's what distinguishes it from deceit. Besides, you have good sense, you grasp things quickly.

LYUBOCHKA. Our old life has become so ridiculous to me. Everything will be special for you and me, with new ideas. That is why I love you.

VENEROVSKY. Lyubov Ivanovna, you couldn't have rewarded me as much with anything else as you did now by saying this. Your entire situation is already becoming ridiculous to you, soon it will disgust you, and then everything will be fine. You understand that the main obstacle for the development of individuality in general is the family, especially for you. All your inclinations are good, but the people around you are lower than the lowest level. There's just one human personality—that is Katerina Matveyevna, and even she, for reasons known to you, is not a well-wisher to everyone now. The rest of them around you are dirt, soiling you.

LYUBOCHKA. Well, why so, Daddy is smart and sympathizes, now Momma is a little bit... But she's so kind, and she loves me so. And Daddy likes you very much...

VENEROVSKY. You do have to distance yourself from them, yes. Of course they love you. Every bad person, no matter how bad he is, wants to be close to a good person. Why then should we love the obsolete and worthless? You have to stay away, away.

LYUBOCHKA (*capriciously*). Don't speak like that. I don't like it, I don't, I don't.

VENEROVSKY. Simply look at them like at strangers, then? You couldn't find them attractive.

LYUBOCHKA. I don't like when you speak that way, I don't. If you say that to me again, I'll completely stop liking the new ideas, and when I marry you, I'll live in my way and not in yours. It'll serve you right.

VENEROVSKY. Well, what is in your way?

LYUBOCHKA. This is what: we'll go to Moscow and rent a very nice house. I'll have one dress made in black velvet and one in white—paduasoy. In the morning we'll go for a ride, then we'll go to Auntie's for lunch, and then I'll put on my black velvet dress and we'll go to the theater, to the boxes. Then I'll put on another dress and we'll go to a ball at my godfather's, and then we'll come home and I'll tell you everything and not read a single book. But I will love you. I will love you very much and not give you any freedom. Because if I fall in love with you, I'll love you so that I'll forget everything except you. Momma was that way, and I take a lot after her. And you'll see how good it'll be! You'll see.

VENEROVSKY. But you'll only do that if I speak that way, right?

LYUBOCHKA. No, I'll simply do it. I'm angry with you.

VENEROVSKY. And is this how you'll fall in love with me?

LYUBOCHKA. Yes, if you'll be sweet. I haven't loved anyone yet, just one person a little. But that doesn't count.

VENEROVSKY (*smiles and takes her hand, indecisive about whether to kiss her*). Yes, to live this way...but...for this you need: first of all—means, secondly—to forget principles...

LYUBOCHKA. Don't speak foolish words! (*Raises her hand toward his lips and presses his cheek.*) That's all nonsense!

VENEROVSKY. Sweetheart... (*Wants to embrace her.*)

LYUBOCHKA. Don't say sweetheart, that's so unpleasant, disgusting...such a word is silly...

VENEROVSKY. Why is it unpleasant? Well, how about—adorable...

LYUBOCHKA. I can't explain... It's unpleasant, awkward. Sweetheart!... It's somehow vile. You don't know how to be tender. (*Smiles.*) Well then, I'll teach you. It's somehow awkward, but I can't say why.

VENEROVSKY. Oh, how charming she is! That's an aesthetic delight!... What am I saying...how foolish...yes... So, do you like me, Lyubinka?

LYUBOCHKA. Yes. But why do you walk like you have sore feet?

VENEROVSKY. What nonsense I'm talking! (*Gets up.*) No, Lyubov Ivanovna, one has to look at life more seriously. Let's take a walk in the garden...

LYUBOCHKA. Okay. (*Exiting, they meet* BEKLESHOV.)

BEKLESHOV (*quietly to* VENEROVSKY). Well, pal, it's done. I've set that damsel Dudkina on the student so that you can't pull them apart.

SCENE 5

Enter MARYA VASILEVNA *and* IVAN MIKHAILOVICH.

IVAN MIKHAILOVICH (*to* BEKLESHOV). I'm happy that Anatoly Dmitrievich entrusted you with talking over the financial matters. I'll tell you and you tell him. I do understand Anatoly Dmitrievich. He is so deeply noble, so tactful, that...

BEKLESHOV. No doubt. I can tell you that I'm a practical man, but in this regard I understand Venerovsky's aversion for this conversation. You know there are always good people who misinterpret everything inside out...

IVAN MIKHAILOVICH. Well yes, yes. We can take this matter up now—

before the guests arrive. Here, have a look... Lyuba's estate is her mother's estate...

MARYA VASILEVNA. I hope, *Jean*, you haven't decided anything without me. *J'espère, Jean, que vous ne déciderez rien sans moi.* I am the mother and the estate is mine.

IVAN MIKHAILOVICH (*astonished*). What's the matter with you? What is it, Marya Vasilevna? (*Quietly.*) Aren't you well? Didn't you and I speak about this already.

MARYA VASILEVNA (*suddenly angered*). After all, I am the mother and before deciding the matter with strangers they should speak with me. As it is, they say that nobody gives a damn about me. I'm treated like a rag. The estate is mine and I won't give anything until I want to. If I want to, I'll give. After all, I should have been asked first. Even decency demands that. Just ask the gentleman. *Rien que les convenances l'exigent—demandez à monsieur.*

IVAN MIKHAILOVICH. I didn't expect that! What's the matter with you? Pull yourself together, come to your senses. Think about what you're saying in front of strangers.

MARYA VASILEVNA. Maybe you don't understand what you're saying, but I understand very well. Everyone says that not much is known about the fiancé.

IVAN MIKHAILOVICH. Not much is known about him! Please, don't talk nonsense!

BEKLESHOV. This is all rather strange, to say the least.

MARYA VASILEVNA. No, I've put up with enough. Everyone says that I'm last in this house. I'll upset the whole wedding!

IVAN MIKHAILOVICH. What's with you? Why? What do you want?

MARYA VASILEVNA. Because I don't know him. I'm not saying anything bad. *Je n'ai pas de dent contre lui,* I just don't want to give any of the estate before the wedding. The Volokolampsk Estate is mine. After the wedding I'll see, if he's a respectful son-in-law, I'll give, otherwise every writer will be...

IVAN MIKHAILOVICH (*sternly, taking her by the hand*). That's enough. Let's go, we'll speak about it there.

MARYA VASILEVNA (*becoming timid*). It's alright, *Jean*, there's no need for

me to go, *laissez moi en repos, au nom du ciel.* Leave me alone for
God's sake. I'm not going to say anything anymore.

IVAN MIKHAILOVICH (*to* BEKLESHOV). Well, as you can see, it's a strange
quirk, but you do understand that it doesn't mean a thing. But I would
ask you not to say anything about this in front of Anatoly Dmitrievich.

BEKLESHOV (*with an air of thoughtfulness*). I understand very well, I'm
afraid I understand too well.

SCENE 6

Enter GENTLEMAN GUEST, LADY GUEST, *followed by* LYUBOCHKA *and*
VENEROVSKY.

GENTLEMAN GUEST. We just found out. How unexpected, my hearty congratulations.

LADY GUEST. What happiness for you, Marya Vasilevna.

IVAN MIKHAILOVICH. Thank you very, very much.

MARYA VASILEVNA. Yes, it was so unexpected. Let me introduce you, here
are the bride and groom.

VENEROVSKY (*looks somberly at the guests and stops*). Yes, Lyubov
Ivanovna, to put up with this repulsive and outrageous banality one
has to really love the thing one has undertaken, and fervently want to
pull you out of the mire and save you. Just look, what is this? And I
have to form relations with these people!

LYUBOCHKA. Well, what does it cost you!

IVAN MIKHAILOVICH. Here he is. (*To* VENEROVSKY.) Please meet my
wife's uncle, my cousin.

GENTLEMAN GUEST. Let me introduce myself as your future relative, my
hearty congratulations. (*Extends his hand.*)

LADY GUEST. I'm very, very happy to meet you, I've heard so much about
you. Congratulations, Lyuba!

VENEROVSKY (*bows, folds his hands behind his back, turns away and walks
over to* BEKLESHOV).

GENTLEMAN GUEST. Such a boor!

LADY GUEST. What strange behavior with relatives!

VENEROVSKY (*to* BEKLESHOV). They and their handshakes! Thay have to be reined in... That they understand well. (*They speak quietly.*)

IVAN MIKHAILOVICH. Please come into the drawing room, besides it's time for lunch. We'll bless the bride and groom.

GENTLEMAN GUEST. Well, have you found a steward, Ivan Mikhailovich?

IVAN MIKHAILOVICH. Don't ask, I'm really struggling... (LYUBA, MARYA VASILEVNA, IVAN MIKHAILOVICH *and* GUESTS *go into the house.*)

SCENE 7

BEKLESHOV *and* VENEROVSKY.

BEKLESHOV. The business with the damsel Dudkina worked out magnificently—I flattered her and the student a little, I divulged love on his behalf and hooked them so that you can't pull them apart. So I nailed her. As concerns finances, matters are really bad. The mother wants to keep a bridle on you and wait to see how respectful the son-in-law is. That's typical. And, I can tell you, the father is no better.

VENEROVSKY. The father is acting nasty. One can forgive him much if that's the only thing.

BEKLESHOV. It would be good if he were thoroughly nasty, but my view, as a practical man, is that this scene was also staged, and the mother only appears to be a fool. That's the partner whom no one sees, who is cruel and hinders the good partner in everything. Well, we've nailed even worse types.

VENEROVSKY. However it's unpleasant that I have to go through these stupid ceremonies as long as this business is so uncertain.

BEKLESHOV. So what of it, do these ceremonies obligate you in any way? I'm telling you, you're an idealist! You keep on thinking how not to behave badly. Get that out of your head, pal; for them there's neither the honest nor the dishonest. Otherwise you'll always be the fool with these folks. Look at things simply. If you had to save a friend from a den of thieves, would you then be afraid of deceiving the thieves? Well, that's how you treat them. The main thing is the wedding itself, and on that memorable day, if not sooner, this old man will be nailed by your most humble servant. You have nothing to worry about. Everything will be carried out in the best form. I give you my word. Well, let's go. (*They begin to go into the house.*)

SCENE 8

THE SAME *and* LYUBOCHKA.

LYUBOCHKA (*comes out*). Let's go, Anatoly Dmitrievich, they're going to bless us. (*Happily.*) Why are you standing here? I also think this is nonsense, but we have to.

VENEROVSKY. I'll be ridiculous and loathsome to myself, yes, ha, ha! Lyubov Ivanovna, I do find this comedy repulsive. You know what my convictions are.

LYUBOCHKA. No, no, no, don't argue! (BEKLESHOV, VENEROVSKY, *and* LYUBOV IVANOVNA *leave for the house.*) This is my month... (*To the* STUDENT *and* PETRUSHA *in the doorway.*) Petya, come quickly, Momma wants you. It's very important.

SCENE 9

THE SAME; *the* STUDENT *and* PETRUSHA *come out, chewing, followed by* KATERINA MATVEYEVNA.

PETRUSHA. Well, why?

LYUBOCHKA. Go, please, you'll find out. (*To* VENEROVSKY.) No, no, Anatoly Dmitrievich, don't argue. Just come. (*All go into the house. Enter the* STUDENT *and* KATERINA MATVEYEVNA. *The* SERFS *run up to the window.*)

The STUDENT *and* KATERINA MATVEYEVNA.

STUDENT. What's all the commotion. Is there some sort of little scandal?

KATERINA MATVEYEVNA. The advocate of women's freedom is marrying a kid, an insignificant and underdeveloped kid. Here is manifested the weakness of his principles.

STUDENT. That's a bit of a surprise, I'd say.

KATERINA MATVEYEVNA (*looking through the window*). Look, look, they are being blessed and are on their knees. That is too repulsive for me to watch, too degrading for human dignity.

STUDENT (*looking*). The *seignior* is trash, I expressed this opinion to you but you didn't share it.

KATERINA MATVEYEVNA. No, listen, it is disgusting, isn't that so?

STUDENT. That's what semidevelopment means. A damned excise liberal!

KATERINA MATVEYEVNA (*looking*). They are kissing—what animal behavior! Yes, looking at such degradation, it is easy to lose one's belief in progress. Now that's a lesson for you, Aleksey Pavlovich. But I am above this. Yes, Aleksey Pavlovich, you are yet another honorable and untainted person among this bunch of rabble. I respect you.

STUDENT. Yes, if only there were more women like you! Nevertheless, they still arranged an estimable celebration!

ACT III

PART 1

Dramatis personae
Ivan Mikhailovich
Marya Vasilevna
Lyuba
Petrusha
Nannie
Katerina Matveyevna
Tverdynskoy
Nikolaev
   a relative of the Pribyshevs, the Marshal of nobility
Best man
First, Second, and Third young lady
Maid
Footman

The Pribyshevs' apartment in a district town. The table is being set up for a gala dinner.

SCENE 1

IVAN MIKHAILOVICH, MARYA VASILEVNA, NANNIE, *and* NIKOLAEV, *a fat landowner-marshal of nobility with a moustache.*

IVAN MIKHAILOVICH. So is the bride getting dressed? That's good. It's time, it's time. It's going on seven.

NIKOLAEV. No, my friend, if I hadn't liked you since we were kids, I wouldn't have agreed to come to this wedding for anything. It's just for you. I don't like that gentleman. And what kind of manners does he have? We waited twice, waited—he didn't show his face. Why? He's the groom and didn't come to meet his bride's relatives! What, does he despise us, is that it?

IVAN MIKHAILOVICH. Ah, what's with you! What do you want from him? He doesn't have any relatives, you know—no one to teach him, besides he's got a lot on his mind... It's not easy, you know, he has to provide everything, arrange everything—he didn't have time to come, somehow. You know, you always get insulted. You're a good but suspicious man.

NIKOLAEV. No, my friend, don't make excuses... Once is all right, but yesterday we waited and waited for him for dinner until six o'clock... He should've said that I, I say, am such an important gentleman and don't want to meet you, then we would've known and started dinner at four; at least we wouldn't have had to eat it rewarmed... No, my friend, I don't like to wait for anyone.

IVAN MIKHAILOVICH. Well, this is the way you explain things. He didn't want to prove anything. He's a remarkable man: intelligent, educated... When you get to know him, you'll speak otherwise. I was saying the same thing until I got to know him. Something simply detained him. Besides, my friend, you have to take into consideration that we're in a different age now, it's not like our time... Different conditions, and many customs are obsolete already.

NIKOLAEV. Just remember my words, you'll have some trouble today... What are you telling me! What about today? We invited him for pancakes, it was the same: we waited until three—he didn't come. Again we had to eat sour pancakes. Just remember my words. I've been thinking, my friend, (*leads him aside*) you didn't by any chance insult him with regard to the dowry? Tell me the whole truth. Have you given him something yet or not?

IVAN MIKHAILOVICH. Well, my friend, to tell you the truth, he hasn't asked me for anything. At first I began to speak about it—he refused. Another time—the same thing: I, he says, don't need anything... Well, and then my old lady acted up... So I decided to wait. I think to myself: he knows that I have an only daughter and I've designated the Volokolampsk Estate for her; I'll see how he'll be to her, and I'll give it on the day of the wedding or the next day. I can tell you, as concerns the dowry, everything is just fine.

NIKOLAEV. What's that, my friend—goodies! The present-day snotnoses go for money even more than we do, they especially like ready cash.

That's not good. You'll see, he'll pull some stunt!

IVAN MIKHAILOVICH. Well, that's nonsense. No, my friend, but what a twenty-year-old madeira I'm going to treat you with, really special!

NIKOLAEV. Just wait a minute, tell me how the ceremony will be. Everything according to custom? So now we'll take the bride to the church, then what?

IVAN MIKHAILOVICH. Then you'll go to his place. As usual, the father and mother won't go. He'll probably serve tea...you know, some candies, fruit for the young ladies, well, some broth in bowls, fish, something in bachelor fashion. Of course, you'll have some champagne there... Then to my place for dinner, and then we'll see them off (they're leaving from my place). We'll have dinner, drink to the health of the newlyweds... (What a madeira we'll have! Hungarian! My father came back with it from the war—forty-five years!)... The carriage will be brought up...the dowry stowed...we'll bless them, and, with God's help, they'll go abroad.

NIKOLAEV. That's a stupid idea, even though it's an English one! The English usually come up with good ideas, but this one is completely foolish. Well, how can you leave right after the ceremony! Well, after all, it's good that you've got lots of money: they'll have a carriage, a maid, and everything else—but what about those who don't have money and go in a wagon and without a maid? It's still bad: instead of letting the bride come to herself, there she is—on the way! bouncing about! It's foolish!

IVAN MIKHAILOVICH. What can you do, my friend! That's the new thing... And in many ways that's also all right. (*Enter the* FOOTMAN *with a basket of silverware and dishes.*) What is it? I sent him to the groom with dishes, with silverware... A bachelor, you know, might not have enough... (*To the* FOOTMAN.) Well, what is it?

FOOTMAN. He said, "I need nothing."

IVAN MIKHAILOVICH. Who said?

FOOTMAN. He himself came out and said: "I don't need it, take it back."

IVAN MIKHAILOVICH. Well, now you see—he's got everything. He had to supply everything, you know. It makes sense that the young man was so busy, doesn't it? (*A* MAID *passes by.*) Well, how goes it, will the bride be ready soon?

MAID. She's having her hair set. (*Exits.*)

FOOTMAN (*enters with a note*). From the groom to the young lady.

IVAN MIKHAILOVICH. What's that? A kerchief... (*Reads.*) "Sweetheart, adorable! So that your precious little throat should not get cold, I am sending you a kerchief, and ask you to wear it." That's strange.

NIKOLAEV. Did he send her a present? Well, a diamond, a shawl, you know, as is customary?

IVAN MIKHAILOVICH. Well, who gives presents now! And why give? It's not the present that counts but love. He gave her a pair of scissors, I think...

NIKOLAEV. Well, you can spit in my face if something nasty don't happen. What's this new way about? You don't get married every day, you know, do you? If you're not happy, at least make the girl happy... You know, this is a great joy for her! But here he sent a two-bit pair of scissors... What the heck! It makes no sense at all... Should I go to the ladies... Ah, here comes the best man. (*Enter* BEST MAN.)

SCENE 2

THE SAME *and* BEST MAN.

IVAN MIKHAILOVICH. Well, what about the groom? Will he be long? We're ready. Lyubochka, will you be long?

LYUBOCHKA (*her voice*). Coming!

BEST MAN. He's wearing a frock coat...

IVAN MIKHAILOVICH. What? How come? You have to tell him that Lyubochka's wearing a white wedding dress. Go right away, tell him...

NIKOLAEV. I said there'd be a scandal... (*Exit* BEST MAN.)

SCENE 3

Enter MARYA VASILEVNA, NANNIE, LYUBOCHKA, PETYA, YOUNG LADIES, *and the* MAID.

LYUBOCHKA. Daddy, do I look pretty?

FIRST YOUNG LADY. Fleur d'orange really becomes you! Will you please give me one from the wreath...

LYUBOCHKA. I'll give 'em to everyone.

SECOND YOUNG LADY. Are you going to put on the groom's kerchief?

THIRD YOUNG LADY. How can you! A print with a white dress!

FIRST YOUNG LADY. What does it matter if he himself is wearing a frock coat?

SECOND YOUNG LADY. That's impossible!

LYUBOCHKA. I'll try it on. He asked me to, so I should wear it. (*Twirls in front of the mirror.*) No, I can't. Well, I'll put it in my pocket.

BEST MAN. Let's get going... Bless her...

NIKOLAEV (*blesses her and kisses her on the forehead*). Well, God bless you! How pretty you are! (LYUBA *kisses everyone; the women cry.*)

SCENE 4

Enter the STUDENT *and* KATERINA MATVEYEVNA. *They stand silently.*

MARYA VASILEVNA. I really hope he won't be late to dinner.

IVAN MIKHAILOVICH. Well, may God bless you!.. Enough, Nannie, it's foolish...

NANNIE (*crying*). I won't see yuh anymore, my little angel!

LYUBOCHKA (*to the* BEST MAN). Will you please not put the crown on my head. But you, Petrusha, put it on him.

MARYA VASILEVNA. Make sure you step on the carpet first. Did you take the candles? Nannie, here's money—throw it under their feet...[11]

NANNIE. I'll take care of it all.

NIKOLAEV. Everything points to a scandal...

IVAN MIKHAILOVICH. Well, thank God... We have to prepare everything now... We're not saying good-bye yet, are we? (*They all exit one at a time except the* STUDENT *and* KATERINA MATVEYEVNA.)

SCENE 5

Katerina Matveyevna *and the* student.

KATERINA MATVEYEVNA. Y..yes. There are still many subjects in whose mind the new ideas are still, so to say, in outline form, and still have not penetrated the heart and soul. Yes, I was cruelly mistaken about that gentleman.

STUDENT. Don't believe lies and you won't be deceived, as our psychology professor used to say. The point is that his character is trash.

KATERINA MATVEYEVNA. Excuse me, excuse me! But how do you explain this phenomenon to yourself? It must be known to every thinking person that an attraction to good looks is simply the lowest manifestation of human nature. How can such a person as this gentleman not see the extreme vileness of this attraction, and the profound depth of his fall! How can he not understand that once you have entered this environment, and subjected yourself to these ingenuous and stifling conditions, there is no return? And he understands woman's freedom, I know for a fact...

STUDENT. By the inclinations of his character he is an insignificant *seignior*, that is all. As soon as I glanced at this person, I became convinced that everything in him is false. Say what you wish—an individual who serves as an excise official, and who has a horse, and an apartment, and a two-thousand-rouble salary is not in any way a new man. He's a new *seignior*, that's all. Why once, in front of me, he called university students "kids"!... That's the understanding of these gentlemen! That entire honorable bunch is trash, just trash, my esteemed Katerina Matveyevna. No, I'm sick of it. I should go to Moscow.

KATERINA MATVEYEVNA. Yes, with your spontaneous feeling you penetrated his character more profoundly than I. I remember now—he told me that introspection is harmful! An insignificant gentleman... And how he lowered himself to a most banal marriage with all the attributes of insignificance! And to whom! To a most insignificant person...

STUDENT. Well, the girl wasn't bad. She still could have developed. She had potential... But her environment cut her short. I'm going to Moscow... I'll attend lectures, I'll work.

KATERINA MATVEYEVNA. Excuse me. In Moscow, you know, they aren't worth attending. All the professors are an undeveloped lot. I myself would go to Moscow or to Petersburg to study physiology... Yes, I share this conviction. But whose lectures? There is no one in Petersburg.

STUDENT. Well, all the same, at least my friends are living persons and not such stale subjects like here.

KATERINA MATVEYEVNA. Yes, you are luckier... But how are we women to arrange our lives? I also thought of going to the university if only I knew for certain, what are those new conditions in which I will find myself? Otherwise, it is difficult for us progressive people to find a path in life on which reactionaryism, stagnation, and obduracy would not crush us. I cannot remain here any longer. I feel that all those honorable and liberal inclinations of my character, those that constitute my strength, are withering here, and I, it is frightening to say, I will soon not exactly resemble these people, but become close to all their principles... What is there to do! Aleksey Pavlovich! You are a broad, vivid, and unspoiled person, you see things more clearly. Save me! Save a perishing, free, perhaps the only completely free woman. Yes, I feel that I am perishing, that light of freedom is growing dim from the ignorance with which I have been living. This man dealt me a horrible blow! He shook my belief in progress. Save me, Aleksey Pavlovich, you are an untainted man, completely a man!...

STUDENT (*moved*). You are such an honorable person!...

KATERINA MATVEYEVNA. No, excuse me! I am perishing, and they will all celebrate! They will all say: there, she wanted to be free—but she is the same as the rest of us. They will be happy. Instruct me, what am I to do?... Of the entire throng surrounding me, I deeply respect you alone!...

STUDENT (*squeezes her hand*). I can say that I didn't know you up to this moment. It seemed to me—I'll be completely frank—that you were not imbued to the core with our convictions. Only now do I see completely all the loftiness and sincerity of your views.

KATERINA MATVEYEVNA (*squeezes his hand very firmly*). Yes, I have thought and suffered a great deal. For me there is no return. I hate backwardness, I am completely dedicated to the new ideas. There is nothing that could stop me, and I respect you, respect you deeply. Instruct me, where to run, where will it be easier for me to breathe. All the surroundings here are suffocating me. I will listen to your advice alone. I am waiting.

STUDENT (*becomes thoughtful*). Yes, I know a circle of people among whom you could occupy that place in life to which you're summoned. Yes. But I'm afraid that you, nevertheless, are toying, that you will be frightened...

KATERINA MATVEYEVNA. Excuse me, excuse me, what makes you say this?

STUDENT. Let me explain. I am also tired of life in Moscow: poverty, an absence of work and regular income. I'm sick of hanging around lecture halls and listening to the dribble of professors—they're a bunch of empty noggins... To teach well-fed nobility brats is even more foolish. I had another type of life in mind. You see, in Petersburg there's a circle of people who began to do something good. They organized a commune. And I also wanted to join these people...

KATERINA MATVEYEVNA (*taking hold of his hand*). Aleksey Pavlovich, do continue! I feel that this commune is composed precisely of those persons whom I seek... Aleksey Pavlovich, I am trembling with excitement... Save me!

STUDENT. Let me explain further: these people live in Petersburg. One of them is my friend. He is from a seminary. (As everyone knows, to be from a seminary these days is almost a rank, since the best minds and talents are all from a seminary.) He is even known in the literary world for his criticism of the tale "Siskins." Perhaps you've read it? An excellent article: "Don't Sissify A Siskin." Here he expresses his thoughts about the progress of ideas in our seminaries.

KATERINA MATVEYEVNA. It is excellent. I read it. Magnificent, a magnificent article.

SCENE 6

PETRUSHA *enters unnoticed and listens.*

STUDENT. Now this gentleman writes to me that they have organized a commune in Petersburg. There were three of them: a doctor, a "nobody," and a student. A most important undertaking. The point is that they joined one another for a common life. They share everything—the apartment, food, income, and expenses. They have a nice apartment, and two women live together with them. Everyone works according to his choice, everyone has his own room, and then there's a common room. The women living with them are not bound by any obligations. They're free, they work...some as housekeepers for men...some follow literary pursuits... Marriage does not exist, relations are completely free. It began small, but now, I was told, they already have about eighteen members in the commune, and it's growing. You understand what enormous significance this must have. In addition, my friend wrote me that there had been some minor dissatisfactions which, however, were settled, but the spirit of this commune is unimaginable. Its members, he writes, become completely different people as soon as they join.

KATERINA MATVEYEVNA. And woman is free?

STUDENT. Completely. There is, however, a dangerous threat from the government, because it's understandable what enormous significance this institution must have. So that is what began, and that is how I could live instead of teaching an overfed nobility brat. I only wish I had some modest means. That's it. I never said anything to anyone about this, because it's too much of an intimate matter. But now I've told you, because I see that you're not toying but have strong convictions...

KATERINA MATVEYEVNA (*smacking herself in the head excitedly*). That is magnificent! Commune—that is a great idea. That is marvelous! Yes, I see the dawn of real progress in Russia. Yes, Tverdynskoy, I am yours!

STUDENT. That's an honorable character! But think it over, it's undoubtedly a very good thing, but...

KATERINA MATVEYEVNA. I am a member of the commune. Write to your friend that two members, you and I, are joining the commune. Now I will take the money I have, go with you to Petersburg, and have Ivan Mikhailovich sell my land and send the money to the commune. I will work on my treatise on the significance of the intellectual activity of women. Tverdynskoy, I was cruelly deceived once already! You will not betray our principles, will you?

STUDENT. I would not respect myself if I could betray them; we'll go, and the sooner the better.

KATERINA MATVEYEVNA. So long, I am going to write to Ivan Mikhailovich. I do not want to see him and will express everything to him in writing.

STUDENT. There is still one bit of nasty business—I took thirty roubles in advance.

KATERINA MATVEYEVNA. I do not have thirty roubles, but I will give him the right to deduct this amount from the sale of my lands.

STUDENT. Without a doubt the step we're taking is so important that such considerations can be put aside. The end justifies the means.

PETRUSHA (*appears*). Let me tell you something: I'm not a well-fed nobility brat, but a person who is trying to understand his calling just as you are. You are very wrong thinking this about me.

STUDENT. I was speaking in general, and not in any way referring to you.

PETRUSHA. And it's ignoble, even nasty! I came to tell you that I, too, do not want to remain in this house. I have thought about my situation and have become convinced that my family is the main obstacle in the development of my individuality. My father is sending me back to school, but I've become convinced that in my development I am above all the teachers. I was just reading Buckle.[12] He says the same thing. I'm going to Moscow.

STUDENT. You'll cause a scandal, that's all. They won't let you.

PETRUSHA. I'm no longer a child. I spoke with father. He insists that I stay in school, but I don't want to and will go alone to Moscow.

STUDENT. Pyotr Ivanovich, you'll only make a major muddle and nothing more... You can't come.

PETRUSHA. I heard your conversation. I want to go with you to the commune, and I'll study the natural sciences. The weight of my father's power is unbearable.

STUDENT. You don't know what you're talking about. You're still too young.

KATERINA MATVEYEVNA. Tverdynskoy, you are forgetting your calling. We do not have the right to crush youthful aspirations seeking freedom and boundlessness. Pyotr Pribyshev, I will propose you for membership in the commune.

PETRUSHA. Katerina, I respect you. When are you leaving? Today? Then I'll get my things ready. I'll just drop by Venerovsky's place: I want to see all of that foul ceremony so that I can be even more indignant.

STUDENT (*to* KATERINA MATVEYEVNA *quietly*). You shouldn't have asked him. He's a kid.

KATERINA MATVEYEVNA. Tverdynskoy, all people are equal, all are free. Let's go, we have to get ready, and have to write letters. Pyotr Ivanovich, explain your convictions to your father.

PETRUSHA. I'm already thinking about the content... The family is an obstacle... (*All exit.*)

PART 2

Dramatis personae
Venerovsky
Lyubov Ivanovna
Bekleshov
Petrusha
The Nikolaevs
   husband and wife
Venerovsky's relative
Best man
High-school boy
First, Second, Third, and Fourth guest

The GROOM's run-down bachelor apartment. Nothing is ready for the guests. Scattered papers. Suitcases.

SCENE 1

BEKLESHOV, *the GROOM's relative—an aged functionary with a decoration in the shape of a cross—and the FOOTMAN are packing.*

RELATIVE. How can one do this, Sergey Pavlovich? They're just leaving like that? That's not the way things are done.

BEKLESHOV. Yes, just like that. That's how it should be. Now they'll return from church, he'll throw on a coat and they'll take off. I did tell you that Anatoly Dmitrievich won't be at all happy to see you, wait and see. If the wedding reception had been here, you know, then fine; but the way it is, they want to do everything as quietly as possible.

RELATIVE. If that's the case, I should leave, you know. However, I feel that I can't hurt my nephew, not even in front of the bride's relatives. Well, if it was his brother, Nikita—that's a disgraceful man, or even my in-law...but me, I'm a Collegiate Councillor, and quite well known. I won't hurt him.

BEKLESHOV. That's not the point, my good sir. This isn't a merchant's wedding, and it's been so arranged that they go straight from the altar to a carriage, and off they go abroad. (*To the* FOOTMAN.) Well, are the horses harnessed? See to it that the key is placed up front. What about the lard? Don't you remember anything without me? Here, take the suitcase. (*To the* RELATIVE.) Oh, you! You're only in the way!... And why did you put on a white tie, a cross!... All that's ridiculous. Look: I'm in a frock coat, and so is the groom.

RELATIVE. I'm leaving, I'm leaving. Just tell me one thing, did Tolya get very much?

BEKLESHOV. What's this Tolya?... The man's thirty-five years old. He got nothing. They cheated him.

RELATIVE. No, you're kidding, aren't you? I know that kinship means nothing to you, but we older people, we thought... You tell me the truth... How's it so, nothing? Ivan Mikhailovich isn't a poor man, you know.

BEKLESHOV (*stops opposite him, aside*). Let him blab around town. (*Aloud.*) This is how they cheated him. He proposed two months ago, they brought up the matter of the dowry, he was too tactful, said he wanted nothing... That's these idealists!

RELATIVE. What foolishness!

BEKLESHOV. Well, so we thought that at any moment they would...we made them feel we were waiting. Nothing. He's embarrassed, says: I'll spoil my reputation, it's more important to me than the dowry...I wanted to have it out with them, he says: wait, wait—and that fool must really have thought that money is not necessary in this new age—and so far he hasn't given him anything. That's what his tactfulness led to!... Ivan Mikhailovich, you're a fine one!.. Well, just you wait...

SCENE 2

Enter the NEWLYWEDS *and* GUESTS. *Congratulations. The* BRIDE *sits down.* VENEROVSKY *walks away.*

VENEROVSKY. Well, is everything ready? (*To his* RELATIVE.) What are you pestering me for with your congratulations, for God's sake! No one asked you to, you know.

RELATIVE. But Tolya, I sincerely mean it. (*Quietly.*) Only I heard that things aren't quite right with the dowry.

VENEROVSKY. What did you hear? What nonsense! I took her without a dowry. (*Walks away.*) God damn them, this stupid company...

SCENE 3

Enter PETRUSHA.

PETRUSHA. Anatoly Dmitrievich, you're a brother to me, but I simply consider you a human being.

VENEROVSKY. Do me a favor, stop this foolishness. What do you want?

PETRUSHA. Father said you should come to dinner as soon as possible; he wants to bless you before you leave... I hope you're not going, are you? It's all so foolish. I don't agree with it. I'm also leaving my father's house.

VENEROVSKY. Good. (*Walks away with* BEKLESHOV.)

BEKLESHOV. Do you see, pal? I told you. Idealists, you don't listen to us practical guys. What now? You have a wife but no money.

VENEROVSKY. The swine!

BEKLESHOV. The game is not lost yet. I'll go and talk things over. You now have two choices: either to go to him and cringe, fawn, wait; or to go and press her. So you choose.

VENEROVSKY. For God's sake, whom do you take me for? Neither the one nor the other. I'll leave as quickly as possible. Well, did you arrange everything?

BEKLESHOV. Yes, rope, lard... We thought of everything... So are you going in the wagon? And you wanted a carriage...

VENEROVSKY. Where do I come to a carriage? We're poor folk; who's there for us to impress, for us it's just "modestly and honestly."

FIRST GENTLEMAN GUEST (*in the crowd*). How come the groom is out of sorts?

SECOND GENTLEMAN GUEST. What's going on? We should congratulate them.

THIRD GENTLEMAN GUEST. Yes, just try, butt in and he'll cut you short...

FOURTH GENTLEMAN GUEST. I'll go and ask him for some champagne.

(VENEROVSKY *lights up a cigarette and paces.*)

NIKOLAEV. Great, real great! (*Goes up to the* BRIDE *and holds her head in his hands.*) Well, once again, congratulations. I'm leaving for your father's... See you there... (*Aside.*) Poor little dear!...

LYUBOCHKA. Wait! Tolya, well, are we going to Daddy?

VENEROVSKY. Please, don't call me Tolya—it's kind of dumb.

LYUBOCHKA. Why are you out of sorts, it seems? For some reason I'm also bored... I didn't expect this at all.

VENEROVSKY (*feigns a smile*). No, I'm all right. (*Sits down next to her.*) It's just that I have a lot on my mind. We have to get ready right away— and now these stupid guests... Why are they here?

LYUBOCHKA. Well, what did you expect, *Anatole*? They're all relatives, friends, you know, only the closest ones, and as it is we insulted so many others! So, are we going to *papa*? And from there straight... When I think that in twelve days we'll be abroad... How wonderful!

VENEROVSKY. I can't go, and we won't go to them. I beg you not to get upset. What are we going to do there? All these ceremonies have worn me out. How could I have possibly endured all of this? So boring!

LYUBOCHKA. Me, too!

VENEROVSKY. Well, of course!

BEST MAN (*approaches*). Anatoly Dmitrievich, the guests wish to congratulate you.

VENEROVSKY. So let them, what's it to me?

BEST MAN. Well, we need some champagne, you know.

VENEROVSKY. Bekleshov, give them some wine—do we have any? Yes, here it is. (*Takes a bottle and puts it on the table.*) Whoever wants, drink. Lyuba, change, it's that time already.

LYUBOCHKA. Well, all right. But where? My Dunyasha isn't here.

VENEROVSKY. Why her? I'll help you, otherwise the cook is here. Please, hurry up! (*Exit* LYUBOCHKA.)

BEST MAN. To the health of the newlyweds!

VENEROVSKY. Drink to whomever's health you want, just be quick about it.

HIGH-SCHOOL BOY (*drinking*). To the health of the freedom of woman!...

VENEROVSKY. Time to go!

HIGH-SCHOOL BOY. And also to the health of science and freedom! Where's the bride? (*The* GUESTS *depart gradually.*) Good-bye, ladies and gentlemen, I'm leaving! To the health of the newlyweds! (VEN-EROVSKY *puts on his coat and hat.*)

LYUBOCHKA (*comes out*). Good-bye, ladies and gentlemen! Give my love to Daddy. Good-bye!

PETRUSHA. I'll see you... I want freedom. They'll really be surprised!

NIKOLAEV. I said there'd be nonsense! That swine! He thinks that it's new... That swine!

HIGH-SCHOOL BOY. I'll have one for the road. So many thoughts!

ACT IV

Dramatis personae
Ivan Mikhailovich
Marya Vasilevna
Nikolaevs
Arbiter
Best man
Guests of both sexes, footmen, musicians

The same room in the Pribyshev home as in Part 1, Act III. The GUESTS *sit in groups.* MARYA VASILEVNA *is dressed up,* IVAN MIKHAILOVICH *is pacing with the* ARBITER.

SCENE 1

MARYA VASILEVNA. What's taking them so long? (*Looks at the clock.*) They should be here!

GENTLEMAN GUEST. They were probably detained. Let's drink to their health! (*Drinks.*) How goes that business of yours?

ARBITER. So this, Ivan Mikhailovich, is your final decision on redemption, isn't it?

IVAN MIKHAILOVICH. I'll give them the Gretsov piece for nothing, and not require any further payment. Well, I think they'll agree.

ARBITER. Why shouldn't they agree, Ivan Mikhailovich. It would be my fault if they reject it. We don't have another example of such generosity, not only in the district, you know, but, I think, in the province... (*A* GUEST *comes up to him.*)

GENTLEMAN GUEST. Even on such a day you have to speak about business?

ARBITER. What else? Whatever you begin to speak about with him, it comes down to the peasants who are to work for him temporarily. Here's an example for you of how things are done. Ivan Mikhailovich is giving the peasants forty-five acres for nothing, and is forgiving payment.

GENTLEMAN GUEST. Is that so!

IVAN MIKHAILOVICH. What's there to do? We have to put an end to it!

ARBITER. That's what time is doing! When one remembers what you said in the beginning, Ivan Mikhailovich! We nearly quarreled then because of that old peasant woman who came to complain, do you remember?...

IVAN MIKHAILOVICH. What else. It was new for me, and I got hot. But how come they're not here yet? It's going on eleven o'clock.

ARBITER. And how the peasants are praising you! And they keep throwing up the example of Mr. Pribyshev to the other landowners.

IVAN MIKHAILOVICH. Yes, that's at least a reward.

ARBITER. Besides, believe me, it'll be more profitable for you, Ivan Mikhailovich.

IVAN MIKHAILOVICH. Well, profitable, hardly, but one has to go along with the times.

MARYA VASILEVNA. He says that it's profitable about everything. He used to say that things have become better because of literacy, and then he gets angry because the peasants don't work. What do you say: are things better because of literacy?

IVAN MIKHAILOVICH. Of course they are. (*Goes up to the* LADIES.) What is it you're speaking about?

MARYA VASILEVNA. We were just reminiscing how we got married. I was telling them how I was afraid of you, do you remember? How you brought a diamond necklace. I didn't want to take it. And then, at the ball: he danced a mazurka with me, and I didn't know whom else to choose... How young and foolish we were! But happy... Momma loved to do it up lavishly. All of Moscow was at our wedding... The entire entrance was covered with red broadcloth and there were two rows of flowers.

SECOND LADY GUEST. No, it wasn't like this at all in the old days.

MARYA VASILEVNA. Now what do we have? A commoner's wedding. Is this really how they would give away an only daughter?

ARBITER. No, not so, you have a very—not exactly gala affair, but *comme il faut*. That's how things are done today, you know: from the altar to the carriage. I find it very good.

MARYA VASILEVNA. But they're still not here.

IVAN MIKHAILOVICH. I also think it's about time. Well, ladies and gentlemen! Help yourself to the wine. I'll bet you've never had anything like it.

MARYA VASILEVNA. *Jean*, explain to me, how are we to meet them? Who will be where? I've forgotten all this already, you know.

SECOND LADY GUEST. As soon as they arrive, Marya Vasilevna, the godfather and godmother must bring them in, and here they are met with bread and salt. At first you...

FIRST GENTLEMAN GUEST. No! This is the way: the best man announces them, and now the godparents enter, and only then the father and mother...

IVAN MIKHAILOVICH. How many rituals there are!

ARBITER. But I like these old ways. It's so good, so Russian.

MARYA VASILEVNA. Please, *Jean*, don't keep them long at the table. I would still like to talk with Lyuba alone.

FIRST LADY GUEST. The joys and the worries, and all this at once... Yes, a memorable time...

IVAN MIKHAILOVICH. Wait! Someone has driven up. Could it be them? Well, get up, Marya Vasilevna, take the bread and salt. This here.

SECOND GENTLEMAN GUEST. Put gold coins in the salt cellar—for a prosperous life.

MARYA VASILEVNA. Ivan Mikhailovich, give me some gold coins.

IVAN MIKHAILOVICH. In a moment! I put them there already. (*The* MAIDS *and* NANNIE *stick their heads out of the doorway; the* MUSICIANS *arrange themselves.*) Mind you, play a flourish when they enter, (*to the* FOOTMEN) and you bring the champagne, and immediately serve the fish...they're coming! (*Takes the bread, puts himself in order, and walks into the middle of the room.*)

FIRST LADY GUEST. What a solemn moment this is!

SECOND LADY GUEST. Especially for the father and mother!

IVAN MIKHAILOVICH (*tearful, he kisses* MARYA VASILEVNA). Well, congratulations, darling. That we've lived to experience such happiness.

MARYA VASILEVNA. Ah, *Jean*, I'm so frightened and so happy, and I myself don't know... You tell me when, otherwise I'll get confused... They're coming!... Should I stand here? (*Footsteps are heard; the* PARENTS *strike a pose, the* RELATIVES *stand around.*)

SCENE 2

Enter NIKOLAEV.

IVAN MIKHAILOVICH. Why aren't you with the godmother? (*Gives a sign to the* MUSICIANS.)

NIKOLAEV. Shsh...blockheads (*to the* MUSICIANS). No, never in my life have I seen such swinishness! (*Throws his hat on the floor.*) I told you, you old fool! No, my friend, I won't let anyone laugh at me. I'm not your relative, not your friend, and I don't want to know you. That's it! (*To his wife.*) Let's go, Sofya Andreyevna.

IVAN MIKHAILOVICH. What is it? What's with him?

MARYA VASILEVNA. Where are the newlyweds? *Jean*, I'm confused.

NIKOLAEV. Yes, go on, kiss him—but go catch up with him!...

IVAN MIKHAILOVICH. What is it then? Don't aggravate me: what's with you? Why?...

NIKOLAEV. They left—that's what! They spit in everyone's face and left. (*Sits down in the armchair, the* GUESTS *surround him.*)

NANNIE. How come, without a blessing?

FIRST GENTLEMAN GUEST. That's not possible!

SECOND GENTLEMAN GUEST. That's unheard of.

MARYA VASILEVNA. Ah! (*Falls into the armchair,* NANNIE *runs over to her.*)

IVAN MIKHAILOVICH (*still holding the bread*). Nikolaev, don't joke around about that... Where is she? I'm talking to you. (*To the* FOOTMAN.) Where are the newlyweds? I'm asking you.

FOOTMAN. They left, sir.

IVAN MIKHAILOVICH. Have you all gone crazy? Did you see them yourself?

FOOTMAN. Of course. Fyodor and I sat them in the wagon.

IVAN MIKHAILOVICH. In the wagon? What wagon? I'll knock your head off, you rascal! (*Moves toward him, throws down the bread, the* FOOTMAN *runs away.*)

MARYA VASILEVNA. *Jean*, what's the matter with you! For God's sake... (IVAN MIKHAILOVICH *stops and becomes thoughtful.*)

NIKOLAEV. Yes, my friend, that's the new way, entirely new. I feel sorry for you, and I find you ridiculous! You go on and be foolish, but don't make fools of others. If I didn't feel sorry for you, I'd drop you and wouldn't say a word.

GUESTS. But what happened? How could they without a blessing!...

ARBITER. How could they go in a wagon? That's not possible...

NIKOLAEV. I knew there'd be some nasty business. I was just waiting. He assured me. I believed him and went to the church. That boor came to the church in a frock coat and blue trousers... Well, fine. I wanted to take her, as one should, according to custom... But he didn't wait for the service to end, grabbed her, sat her in his carriage. Well, I think... I had absolutely no desire to go, but Sofya Andreyevna insisted... We should go, why should we hurt Lyuba... He just doesn't know the custom... Well, I think, I'll go, I feel sorry for Lyuba.

IVAN MIKHAILOVICH. Nikolaev, are you joking?... Where are they? For God's sake, have pity on me... I'm a father, you know...

NIKOLAEV. Why joke, my friend? I wish it was... They're probably at the Lashevo station.

IVAN MIKHAILOVICH. Well, go on, go on...

NIKOLAEV. I think, I should do it for an old friend, although I knew there'd be some nasty business. But, I think, what of it? Some snot nose scribbler can't insult me: I set off. Fine. Sofya Andreyevna and I hurried over to his place—no one there, just the best man... His apartment—a pigsty is cleaner!—rope all over the floor, and some friend of his, a boor just like him, in something like a dressing gown, and a relative—some minor official. What do you think? The groom turned his back to me, walked away, put on his hat, and off they go!

IVAN MIKHAILOVICH. What did they go in?

MARYA VASILEVNA. Without a maid? Dunyasha is here. Oh, my God!

IVAN MIKHAILOVICH. What did they go in? Stab me! here! draw my blood!...

NIKOLAEV. In a wagon, with mats. I saw it myself...

IVAN MIKHAILOVICH. Nikolaev!... Take care...

NIKOLAEV. What's there for me to take care? You should've taken care to whom you gave your daughter...

MARYA VASILEVNA. Was Petrusha there?... What's going on?

SECOND GENTLEMAN GUEST. Probably they insulted him somehow?

THIRD GENTLEMAN GUEST. No. They gave him everything before the wedding, they say.

FIRST GENTLEMAN GUEST. Surely a madman. Believe me, he's a madman.

SECOND GENTLEMAN GUEST. One thing is surprising: how she agreed.

THIRD GENTLEMAN GUEST. He took her in hand.

FIRST GENTLEMAN GUEST. That's a good lesson for Ivan Mikhailovich.

SECOND GENTLEMAN GUEST. All because of his pride.

IVAN MIKHAILOVICH. Was Petrusha there? Hey, Sashka!

MARYA VASILEVNA. *Jean*, for God's sake...

IVAN MIKHAILOVICH. Get out of here!...

FOOTMAN (*enters*). What is it, sir?

IVAN MIKHAILOVICH. Where's Pyotr Ivanovich?

FOOTMAN. I don't know, sir...

IVAN MIKHAILOVICH. I'll teach you to know! Get me Pyotr Ivanovich right now, do you hear, you bandit? (*Suddenly angered.*) I'll teach you to laugh at me! (*The* FOOTMAN *runs away.*)

SECOND FOOTMAN (*enters with letters*). Pyotr Ivanovich left with Katerina Matveyevna and the student, I was told to give the letters directly to you.

IVAN MIKHAILOVICH. What? (*Takes the letters.*) Where did they go? When did they leave?

SECOND FOOTMAN. I don't know, sir. To Petersburg, they said.

FIRST GENTLEMAN GUEST. That's surprising!

SECOND GENTLEMAN GUEST. Yes, misery likes company.

NIKOLAEV. That's the new ideas for you... Now you've really done it.

IVAN MIKHAILOVICH (*opening a letter*). Ladies and gentlemen, this is too hard on me. Have pity on me! I know I'm guilty. There's nothing to hide... I can't read it... Why don't you read it. (*Looks over the letter and hands it to the* BEST MAN.) Go on... Hey, wait! (*To the* FOOTMAN.) Get the four grey ones harnessed to the carriage! And tell coachman Filka that if the carriage isn't here in a minute, he won't have a tooth left in his mouth. I'll knock 'em all out. I'm saying this in front of everyone, and then let God and the Tsar judge me! No, your time has passed! Well, read it.

BEST MAN (*reading the letter*). "Mr. Pribyshev:"

IVAN MIKHAILOVICH. Who's that from?

BEST MAN. From Katerina Matveyevna.

IVAN MIKHAILOVICH. Fine, we'll also settle scores with that damn fool. Go on.

BEST MAN (*reading*). "Although the budding social tendencies that manifested themselves of late more clearly in your person did give us the feeling that you have begun to disturb the peace of the dense self-satisfaction of the ultraconservative and, I would even say, ultrareactionary environment in which you circulated, and did give us hope for a sharp turn in your tendencies toward the new doctrine—a triumph of mind is still not a triumph of deed. To put it simply: the immeasurable gulf separating us from your family made itself felt with diabolical force, subjectively speaking. The recent events in your midst brought out into the open the bastion of ignorance, depravation, and obduracy concealed in it. We were forcibly grouped and therefore could not merge. We were all apart. I have decided to return to Petersburg under a banner which is closer to my heartfelt convictions, under the banner of the new doctrine on woman. Since a turn toward an honorable path was noted in your consciousness, I assume that you will be interested to know about the progress of our activity for the benefit of the general cause, which has an entirely realistic nature. Some progressive persons, honorable individuals, are conducting an experiment in free cohabitation of men and women on a new, original basis. This institution is called a commune. I am becoming a member of it"...

NIKOLAEV. Well, my friend, that's a long-known institution and it's simply called a ... (*Whispers in his ear.*)

IVAN MIKHAILOVICH. Go on reading... Is there much more?

BEST MAN. No, almost finished. (*Reading.*) "Living in the conducive environment of the commune, I will participate in the literary enterprise and promote, to the best of my ability, the ideas of our age, both theoretically and concretely. I will be free and independent. Good-bye, Pribyshev. I do not reproach you for anything. I know that the dirt from your environment could not but besmirch you as well; I am not speaking about Marya Vasilevna; you had to be what you are. But remember one thing: there are clear-minded persons who do not submit to the blows of our age, and upon them you must look, if you do not wish to lose your dignity as a man, upon these persons you must look with feeling and repect. I will be candid—I do not respect you, however I do not absolutely deny the human tendencies in you. I am above making reproaches!"

IVAN MIKHAILOVICH. Is that all? Just you wait!

BEST MAN. No... P.S.: "I request that you sell my land and, I assume, for no less than eighteen roubles an acre—I rely on your honesty—and to send me two thousand, three hundred roubles in silver as soon as possible. By the next post I request that you send me one hundred fifty roubles from my income."

IVAN MIKHAILOVICH. Perfect! She's already taken two hundred and the entire estate pays a hundred fifty. You'll sure hear from me, little lady! Well, next one: probably from the student. Read it.

NIKOLAEV. She's mad! She ought to be put on a chain. And you keep on praising her doctrine.

BEST MAN. "Ivan Mikhailovich: I took an advance of thirty-two roubles from you. I cannot pay them back now. But if you are not a dishonest gentleman, then you will not be base enough to blame me. I will send you money as soon as I can. Wealthy people make a habit of despising poor ones. This was done much too brazenly in your home. I am going with Katerina Matveyevna. Think what you wish about her, but I consider her a lofty person. Anyway, my respects."

IVAN MIKHAILOVICH. Well, short and to the point. Are the horses ready? I'll ride the four of them into the ground but I'll catch up, and at least enjoy myself.

MARYA VASILEVNA. Really, Ivan Mikhailovich! Have pity on him! After all, he's poor, alone.

FIRST GENTLEMAN GUEST. Is there something to pity!

IVAN MIKHAILOVICH. Well, now for the last one... Finish me off...

BEST MAN (*reading*). "Father: I have given a great deal of thought to the philosophy of our age. And it all turns out that people of the new age have a bad life because reactionaries oppress them. Everyone agrees that family hinders the development of individuality. I have already acquired very considerable development, but you are ultraconservatives, and Momma is a fool; you said so yourself, which means, everyone is aware of this. Why should I lose a broad horizon and stagnate? In school the teachers are not as yet developed, and I can't bear it! They put you in a detention room!... Oblomovitis[13] has already passed, new beginnings for progressive people have already begun. I will pursue science at the university in Petersburg if the professors are good; if they are bad, I will work on my own. And if you are not a Kirsanov,[14] not a stupid, willful petty tyrant, then send me the means to live in Petersburg. I have decided already. And I have also become convinced that Venerovsky is a reactionary as well. He does not recognize the freedom of women. Good-bye, Father. Perhaps we will meet as man to man, in a new and normal relationship. I have said everything that was pent-up in my soul. Pyotr Pribyshev."

MARYA VASILEVNA. My God! My God! What's that all about!

NIKOLAEV. Sorry, I feel sorry for you, my friend Ivan, but there's nothing to do, you yourself are at fault. That's the new for you! What's new here!—it's all old, very old: pride, pride, and pride! From the beginning of the world the young want to instruct their elders.

FIRST GENTLEMAN GUEST. That's right.

SECOND GENTLEMAN GUEST. But how far they've gone!

FIRST GENTLEMAN GUEST. It's foolish and ridiculous.

IVAN MIKHAILOVICH. Well, you, Marya Vasilevna, are foolish, but I'm a thousand times more foolish than you. Hey! Is the carriage ready?

FOOTMAN. They're bringing it, sir.

IVAN MIKHAILOVICH. Tell Dunyasha to get ready, she's coming with me. Wait, where is it, the deed? Well, ladies and gentleman, forgive me, I'm going! (*Says good-bye to the* GUESTS.)

ARBITER. So, Ivan Mikhailovich, what about our business?

IVAN MIKHAILOVICH. This is what. Not until they put a knife to my throat will I give away for nothing a single patch of land, nor will I forgive a single kopeck, a single day, or a single penalty! Enough of my surprises! No, I'm well schooled now. No sir, my dear fellow, enough playing the fool.

FOOTMAN. Everything is ready, sir.

IVAN MIKHAILOVICH. My coat, you son of a bitch! What do you think? It's going to be like it was? You're right, Marya Vasilevna, everything has become worse. The regulating charters,[15] and the schools, and the students... It's all poison, it's all ruination. Good-bye. If only I could catch them, at least on the way. I'll really unburden my soul then. I'll give Petrushka a whipping! Yes.

MARYA VASILEVNA. Ivan Mikhailovich, have pity on me, don't yell too much at Aleksey Pavlovich, really. He's so thin, pitiful! He did it because he's so young...

NIKOLAEV. You'll get your son back, but you can't unmarry your daughter!

IVAN MIKHAILOVICH. Better not say anything. (*Goes over to the table and drinks a glass of wine.*) Yes, yes—I'll whip him, whip him with birch rods. Good-bye. You can laugh, scream, be angry, but I'll whip 'im, I will! He himself will say thanks, yes he will!

ACT V

Dramatis personae
Pribyshev
Venerovsky
Lyubov Ivanovna
Katerina Matveyevna
Pyotr Ivanovich
Tverdynskoy, the student
Stationmaster
Overseer
Dunyasha, the maid

The set depicts a room for travelers at a post stage.

SCENE 1

Enter the STATIONMASTER *and* OVERSEER.

STATIONMASTER. What a rush! Hasn't been this way since Holy Makar's day. Whose turn is it?

OVERSEER. Akimka's; he's not back yet. Probably got held up at Lapshevo. We're lucky the courier's not ridin' yet.

STATIONMASTER. And the mail's comin' again after six—what can you do? The travelers are gonna be a pain now.

OVERSEER. That's how things were in the old days when Tikhon Moseich was around: as soon as there weren't no horses, he takes off and hides in the hayloft. I was the overseer then also. Once two drunks were comin' from the Cowcasus, they were comin' and what all didn't they do! They beat up on us all, and everyone at the station run off. They dragged ol' Tikhon Moseich out by the feet. "Don't yuh dare—I'm an official!" So now they really gave it to 'im! Can you believe it, dragged 'im around the yard. I'll tell yuh, we really laughed!

STATIONMASTER. If that kind would get on me, I'd fix 'im.

OVERSEER. No, travelers nowadays have calmed down a lot. How come, I wanted to ask yuh, your honor, nowadays travelers just speak to us peasants like equals.

STATIONMASTER. Well, education, progress. What are yuh, a fool?

OVERSEER. Only us guys noticed, if someone makes yuh an equal that way—don't bother waitin' for a tip. But someone who makes more of a racket and's free with his hands—that one'll give. So wait a bit—either couple of dimes or two bits.

STATIONMASTER (*laughing*). Look who notices!... Enough of that idle chatter. What a filthy mess here. Have them sweep up, and yuh could at least wipe off the table. There ain't a traveler, yuh know, who wouldn't be annoyed. Everything's dirty for 'em. And who is it that makes the mess? They do it all. They just mess everything up on purpose and leave. And everything's dirty for 'em. (*The* OVERSEER *cleans up.*) Should I go take a nap? Not again! Well, they'll have to wait, don't yuh get angry.

OVERSEER. Let 'em pay double, our guys'll drive 'em. (*The sound of a bell.*)

SCENE 2

THE SAME; *enter* VENEROVSKY *and* LYUBOV IVANOVNA, *who is very pale, quiet, and sad.*

VENEROVSKY. Mr. Stationmaster, I require horses. Overseer, have them harnessed quickly. (*To* LYUBOV IVANOVNA.) So now we are alone. Magnificent! Only now do I feel like a person, now that we have broken away from all that hideous nonsense! Are you happy, my sweetheart?

LYUBOCHKA. Don't say those words in front of strangers.

STATIONMASTER. All the horses are out.

VENEROVSKY. I'm telling you, here's my order for them, here's the money, harness the horses.

STATIONMASTER. When they're fed, they'll be harnessed.

VENEROVSKY. Have them harnessed now or else give me the book, I will complain.

STATIONMASTER. Here's the book; complain. There are a lot like you!

VENEROVSKY. Ah, good, very good! For a long time coming honesty will be an attribute of us alone... These rotten little people! (*Sits down at the table, opens the book, and writes.*)

STATIONMASTER (*coming up to him, angrily*). Will you please read the book first. Here, take a look—"mail, 5:23, 8 horses." It's only nine now, they haven't come back. "Colonel and wife, 6:17, 6 horses." Look here—in all there are thirty-six horses. So that's how it is, sir, first look and then call those who are perhaps better than you rotten people—yes sir.

VENEROVSKY. Leave me alone. I don't intend to squabble with you.

STATIONMASTER (*walking off*). You'd better be careful from now on! We won't take that even from a general in a coach and six...let alone some scum... (*Exits.*)

SCENE 3

THE SAME *without the* STATIONMASTER.

VENEROVSKY. Overseer, bring me a samovar please. (*To* LYUBOV IVANOVNA.) Will you have tea, sweetheart? Some tea and sugar!

OVERSEER. The samovar's twenty kopecks, and settle up with the housekeeper for the tea, for the sugar.

VENEROVSKY. Bring it all. Will you have some?

LYUBOCHKA. Yes... No...

VENEROVSKY. Shouldn't you take your cloak off?

LYUBOCHKA. I don't want anything.

VENEROVSKY (*sits down next to her*). Now you see, my dear, what a clear line separates us from your former relatives. We will look at life simply. That gentleman, by virtue of his convictions, his environment, considered it necessary to oppress people and be rude. That is the order of things, just as your relatives consider those foolish proceedings from which we have escaped inevitable. Well, we cannot remake them, can we? But we, as intelligent people, should say: you, ladies and gentlemen, are vile and rotten, but that's your affair; just allow us to be honorable and humane! When you adopt this view, my sweetheart...

LYUBOCHKA. Don't say, "sweetheart"—it's not nice.

VENEROVSKY. Well, it doesn't matter. Just note how in all these conflicts the rotten people are humiliated. I do not hate them, I despise them, they should be humiliated, and they know it themselves when they reflect on it. Believe me, your relatives now feel that they are foolish. That's what is needed.

LYUBOCHKA. What did my relatives do to you? Suppose they are undeveloped, they're still all right. There are a lot worse.

VENEROVSKY. You are very smart, sweetheart. That is so. There are worse, but once we realize that our convictions are different, that the ground on which I and they stand is not one and the same, and we have to take different paths. It's all very simple, you know. I don't respect foolish and uneducated people who are also dishonest, apathetic, and enemies of everything new. And such are your relatives—therefore, neither you nor I can respect them. You agree with this, don't you? Another might begin to dodge, hide his convictions, but I consider honesty and truth to be advantageous always.

LYUBOCHKA. Why? My father is not an enemy of everything new, on the contrary...

VENEROVSKY. Well, can't you see that he was only afraid of me, and was hypocritical. Also, one cannot respect a foolish woman who doesn't understand anything except eating and sleeping!

LYUBOCHKA. Still I loved them...

VENEROVSKY. Love the honorable, the free and the wise! Love those persons who combine these qualities in them, and you will be humane; but to love a woman because she brought you into the world makes no sense. Yes, my most marvelous dear! If you also love me, it's not because I'm good or intelligent, but only because I combine in myself those qualities of which I spoke. Yes, that is so. (*The samovar is brought.*) Will you pour?

LYUBOCHKA. No, I don't want to—it's all dirty and disgusting... Look at these cups—I don't want to.

VENEROVSKY. Yes, Lyubov Ivanovna, my sweetheart, my little wife. A knowledge of all that I have told you comes to others through work and struggle and intense study, and at that only rare and strong individuals master this doctrine as completely and thoroughly as I have, but all this comes easy to you, my lucky one, my sweetheart. You only have to listen, grasp, and you are immediately at that height to which a person of the new age must rise. Let's stop arguing! We are now alone and free. (*Moves closer to her.*) Why aren't you drinking, my little darling?

LYUBOCHKA (*frowning*). What cups! Disgusting! Everyone drank here—sick people maybe. I don't want to.

VENEROVSKY. May I kiss you, sweetheart? I'd like to.

LYUBOCHKA. No... Leave me alone...

VENEROVSKY. You're not in a good mood today. Aren't you happy, my dear, that we're going?

LYUBOCHKA. I don't care, I'm just tired... Why didn't you take Dunyasha?

VENEROVSKY. Again! I don't believe I have the right to bother you with questions. You are as free as I am, and in the future it will also be so... Another might believe that he has rights over you, but I acknowledge your complete freedom. Yes, dear, your life will be so arranged that soon you will say to yourself: yes, I've come out of prison into the light.

LYUBOCHKA. Why didn't you take Dunyasha?

VENEROVSKY. That would have been haughty, wretched, and she would have been in the way. (*Moves closer.*) May I kiss you now?

LYUBOCHKA. Leave me alone! Why don't you wash out the cups, they're so dirty!

VENEROVSKY (*smiling*). That doesn't matter. (*Pours tea and drinks.*) Well, may I kiss you? You tell me when I may. Do you want to rest? I'll leave. I'll never get in the way of your freedom.

LYUBOCHKA. No... Yes... No... I don't want anything. I'm sick of it.

VENEROVSKY. Perhaps you think I didn't foresee such an eventuality. On the contrary. We progressive people are not only good at turning a phrase. There are such types. No, we are people of action. We don't get carried away. I knew you would be bored. If you want, I'll tell you why. Don't be surprised that I guessed, there's nothing surprising about it. You grew up in wretched surroundings. You have a good character, but you have absorbed much in your life from that apathetic and stale atmosphere. Imperceptibly it permeated you. You didn't notice this before, just as you don't notice filth in a pile of manure, but when you came into contact with something pure and strong, the filth became noticeable to you yourself, and the light hurts your eyes. Looking at me, you sense your stain... (*Paces back and forth nervously.*)

LYUBOCHKA (*quietly*). Ah, only about himself!...

VENEROVSKY. What?

LYUBOCHKA. Nothing... Go on.

VENEROVSKY. Don't be afraid of that, my sweetheart: that's a passing sensation. Those who come out of the dark at first think that the light is unpleasant, it hurts. But this sensation is inherent in every radical change. Don't be afraid, but, on the contrary, tear this frailty out by the root. Why are you bored? You feel uncomfortable in the wagon, and you don't have your maid, and you think these cups here are dirty... All this is gentlefolk apathy. Just think, before you is a life of freedom, before you is a man, who for you, for your beautiful eyes, has made every concession to banality that he could, that...

LYUBOCHKA. You only keep on praising yourself...

VENEROVSKY. I praise that which merits praise, I censure that which merits censure, and it's all the same to me whether the good or bad is in me or in you. So-called modesty is one of those preconceptions that is supported by ignorance and stupidity; take your mother who says about herself: I'm a fool. Well, that's all right for her, ha, ha!

LYUBOCHKA. Leave me alone, I'm sick of it.

VENEROVSKY. Well, I'll be quiet, I'll read awhile. It will pass. Perhaps it's because your gallbladder has not emptied its contents. It will pass, there are physical remedies for this. But I will never be angry with you. Whatever you do, I will only seek the cause—find it and remove it. I'll be quiet, and you drink some water. (*Lies down on the sofa, takes a book from his bag and reads.*)

LYUBOCHKA (*gets up and walks over to the door, and asks in the doorway*). Is there a woman here? May I come in? (*A voice from behind the door says: "Welcome." LYUBOCHKA exits. The sound of a bell, voices.*)

SCENE 4

VENEROVSKY, KATERINA MATVEYEVNA, TVERDYNSKOY, *and* PYOTR IVANOVICH, *then the* STATIONMASTER *and* OVERSEER.

OVERSEER (*his voice from behind the scene*). I'm telling you, no horses.

KATERINA MATVEYEVNA (*her voice from behind the scene*). Excuse me, excuse me, you say there are no horses. So why is this place called "post stage"? A stage is for horses, yes or no? (*They all enter;* PETRUSHA *has the hiccups.*)

OVERSEER. I'm telling you, they're all out, there are two people sittin' and waitin' already. (*After noticing the new arrivals,* VENEROVSKY *exits unnoticed.*)

KATERINA MATVEYEVNA. Excuse me, you are not answering my question. By virtue of what are you refusing people who have the identical rights of any general?

PETYA. Hic!... You know...hic!...we're going to Petersburg...hic!... We're locals, you know...hic!... Pribyshevka is ours...hic!... Give us horses, otherwise...hic!...it's really lousy of you...hic!...

OVERSEER. Lemme get the Stationmaster. (*Wants to exit.*)

TVERDYNSKOY (*doesn't let him*). My dear bumpkin: as far as I can conclude from your words, you wish to conduct a commercial operation, but we do not wish to assist it.

OVERSEER. Enough playin' around, sir, just leave me be... (*Enter* STATIONMASTER.)

KATERINA MATVEYEVNA. Allow me to request horses for us. We have full right to them, the same as any official. Here is my permission—how do you call it... The time has now passed when only generals were respected, and the intellectual class, students, despised.

STATIONMASTER. It's over two hours since we've had any horses—please look at the book, and for us all are equal. I also, like everyone else, understand the present age.

PETYA (*to* KATERINA MATVEYEVNA). No, let me...hic!... I'm convinced... I can... (*To the* STATIONMASTER.) Just think...hic...when are we going to get to Petersburg?...hic!...if at every stage...hic!... You know we really have to...hic!...really, please give...figure out how much it'll cost!

TVERDYNSKOY (*to the* OVERSEER). Tell Automedon,[16] in other words the coachman, to bring the small suitcase and white bread. Figure out how much it'll be...there's a bottle there...and you be so good as to give us horses.

KATERINA MATVEYEVNA. Excuse me, I will prove it to you. It would seem that in the present age it should be understood that a woman has the same rights.

STATIONMASTER. Here, would you like to have a look at the book?

PETYA (*to* KATERINA MATVEYEVNA). Don't interfere...hic!... I'll prove it to him...hic!... You know we're going to the com...hic!...mune...

STATIONMASTER. Wherever you like, it's absolutely all the same to me...

TVERDYNSKOY (*takes the book*). As described here in this little book of yours, ostensibly Lieutenant Stepanov was distressed by a delay, since he was in a hurry on business.

KATERINA MATVEYEVNA. I will complain.

STATIONMASTER. Go ahead, madam. There are no horses, that's all there is to it.

KATERINA MATVEYEVNA. But what a lack of understanding of one's duties there still is, and inhumanity.

TVERDYNSKOY. Let me describe in this little book all the stress of our emotional state, and explain the homicidal morals of post stages' stationmasters.

PETYA. No, let me... I have a thought...hic!...

STATIONMASTER (*takes the book away*). Why, ladies and gentlemen, are you actually poking fun at me! I'm as good as you. You want to write, then write, but just act normally.

TVERDYNSKOY. And so, Katerina Matveyevna, a contemptible barrier has slowed down our advance toward the light of progress. This citizen's ire is up, let's leave him be.

PETYA. Hic...hic...hic!... (TVERDYNSKOY *laughs at him.*)

TVERDYNSKOY. I told you, you put away too much of that medicinal Hungarian elixir.

PETYA. What?...hic!...what's so funny?... On the contrary...I won't let you make fun...hic!...

TVERDYNSKOY. What childishness to take offense at everything.

PETYA. You're a child yourself...hic!... I'm a free...hic!...man, hic!... I myself said...I'm...hic!...going to the commune...

TVERDYNSKOY. Go to sleep, Pribyshev junior, it'll be for the better.

PETYA. I expressed the conviction that you're a child...hic!...not I. You don't recognize...hic!...the freedom of an individual, hic!...there... It was only stupid of me to drink that wine...hic!...and it made me sick...hic!...otherwise I would state...hic!...hic!...such convictions to you, that you would be very surprised...hic!... I want to go to sleep. (*Sits down and falls asleep. In his sleep.*) Barrier...hic!...indi...vid...u... hic!...hic!...

TVERDYNSKOY. Well, we'll wait. It would be nice to do some tea-drinking. Otherwise, it's boring. Someone there was drinking. Hey bumpkin, Overseer, Mr. Overseer, can't we get an appliance, called a samovar in everyday speech?

KATERINA MATVEYEVNA (*sits down at the table, lights a cigarette, and brushes her hair back*). I like this playful attitude to life in you, Aleksey Pavlovich. However significant the events taking place in your life, you hide the profound depth of your consciousness in the innermost recesses of your heart, and on the surface you keep on joking. Many may consider you frivolous, but I do like this. I respect you for this. Yes, now we have taken the first step in our new life.

TVERDYNSKOY. Yes, we have. Why all the rhetoric! When you know that your cause is good, that you're free and sensible, what else is necessary? I don't like to prepare. When a cause arises—I'm a toiler and fighter, but before that time...you can indulge in light jesting.

KATERINA MATVEYEVNA. Tell me one thing: I have been thinking all the way here. Why is the founder of the commune a man and not a woman? Does this not here show the idea of dependence of woman?

TVERDYNSKOY. No, pure chance. (*The samovar is brought.*) So, who's going to produce the tea product?

KATERINA MATVEYEVNA. Excuse me, I assume there is as much basis for me to pour as there is for you. I'll tell you what: let's leave it to chance.

TVERDYNSKOY. So we'll entrust the solution of this question to born-blind Fortuna. (*Takes a cigarette and hides it behind his back. KATERINA MATVEYEVNA takes a teaspoon and does the same.*)

KATERINA MATVEYEVNA. No, you guess.

TVERDYNSKOY (*grasps her arm, looks around quickly, and runs his fingers over her arm*). By the way, the plumpness of your arm is not at all bad, so to speak. In this one.

KATERINA MATVEYEVNA (*smiling*). Tverdynskoy, don't be silly. You guessed right. I will pour.

TVERDYNSKOY. How a trip, nevertheless, can bring people closer. It's such a strange feeling to be close to a woman. (*Sits down closer.*) And how nice it is that you're not wearing a crinoline, and what a cute crease you have here, quite classic. (*Points to her back.*)

KATERINA MATVEYEVNA. Tverdynskoy, do you know Hugo's poems? Hugo[17] was a reactionary, but through his poetic instinct he perceived much of the future. *N'insultez pas...*

TVERDYNSKOY. Such a cute crease, first class. Permit me to stroke it lightly, not really stroke it, but just lightly. (*Touches her.*)

KATERINA MATVEYEVNA (*smiles and slaps his hand*). Tverdynskoy, when I know you better, I will tell you about my lot. A woman's lot is a strange abnormality in our undeveloped society. (*Moves aside.*) Tverdynskoy, if I had less respect for you, I could doubt the sincerity of your convictions. What is your hand doing?

TVERDYNSKOY. Aren't the incidents that take place rather strange after all. You and I lived under one roof, for three months, and all the time we spoke about thought-evoking subjects, and now, in an instant, my view of you has changed completely. Why don't you want me to put my hand this way? (*Places his hand on the back of the armchair in which* KATERINA MATVEYEVNA *is sitting.*) I won't touch anything without permission. Anything.

KATERINA MATVEYEVNA (*beaming*). Look into the depths of your consciousness, and then I will honestly hear out your confession. I do not want affairs, we must place ourselves above them. Don't touch me.

TVERDYNSKOY. I'm not touching, I'm not touching anything. You have something consuming in your glance, something beyond the feminine. One of my acquaintances had a friend, a woman, she was a governess. Vavochka was what we called her. You're like her, very much so. But what a nice crease... (*Grabs her and presses her to him.*)

KATERINA MATVEYEVNA. Excuse me, excuse me, think hard and carefully, delve into yourself! The way in which... Tell me, by which love do you love me? (*Tears herself away from him and stands up.*)

TVERDYNSKOY (*walking after her*). You're the incense of my heart, you're the narghile of heavenly hope, you're the fume from the soles of my idols, all the tenderness and light of the universe's firmament. I love you, and wish to make a declaration to you.

KATERINA MATVEYEVNA. Don't speak nonsense, you are insulting me not as a woman but as an honest person. I do not differentiate. You say you are attracted to me, I consider you a nice gentleman; examine the nature of your attraction and tell me. Try to look at things objectively. The concrete can confuse[18] you. I have had my say.

TVERDYNSKOY (*comes closer and seizes her arm*). Divine but free woman! Fortune is favoring us. Minerva's young charge here (*pointing to the sleeping* PETYA) slumbers in Morpheus' embrace, we're alone, and I'm consumed by love. (*Seizes her and wants to kiss her.*) The future is in the hands of fate, the present is ours. (*Embraces her.*) Just stop it, sweetie!

KATERINA MATVEYEVNA (*frightened, she struggles free*). You're insulting me, I'm mistaken in you, too. I'll start screaming, let go!

PYOTR (*in his sleep*). The family...hic...is a barrier...to...in...di...vidu... hic!...ality.

TVERDYNSKOY (*lets her go, angrily*). Now that's unworthy of the truly free woman—to understand everything so grossly...

KATERINA MATVEYEVNA. My God, what have I come to!... My God!... But I'm above... No... I'm lower than everything in the world. I'm a pitiful creature, to me you're vile, but I'm even viler! (*Crushed,* KATERINA MATVEYEVNA *sits down at a distance and gets lost in thought.*)

SCENE 5

THE SAME, VENEROVSKY, *and* LYUBOCHKA.

LYUBOV IVANOVNA (*comes out all in tears*). What kind of freedom of woman is this if you harass me!.. I'm sick of it, how right momma wa... Katinka! Aleksey Pavlovich! My goodness, and Petrusha! What has happened?

TVERDYNSKOY. Not a bad little surprise! Me... I'm also going to Petersburg.

KATERINA MATVEYEVNA. Lyubov! You were right. But leave me alone, I have a lot to think about. (*Sits down at the table, leans on her elbows and thinks.*)

PETRUSHA (*awakens suddenly and stands up*). Wait, I'll tell everything better. You yourself must know that the family...hic!...to the development of individu...hic!...ality. So I left by myself, and Aleksey Pavlovich let out that there's also a commune...and the commune...is a wonderful convic... I mean, institution, well, doesn't matter... I really want to go to sleep, wake me up... (*Sits down.*)

LYUBOCHKA. What's with him?

VENEROVSKY. Nothing special. It's very clear. The kid drinks himself silly and something unspeakably nasty pops up.

PETRUSHA (*half-rising*). You yourself are unspeakably nasty, just everyone knows you're a reactionary, Aleksey Pavlovich, and Katinka told me on the way that you married for money. That's real low in our v... (*Falls asleep.*)

TVERDYNSKOY. Of course he's a kid. Believe me, Anatoly Dmitrievich, I didn't say that and don't think it, because your convictions...

VENEROVSKY. Right, make a mess and then back off! That's just like you. And you, madam, allow me to get to the bottom of things. (*To* KATERINA MATVEYEVNA.) When I explained myself to you, ha, ha! in my apartment, I asked you to remain silent about my person. You promised me this. However you, obviously, are not pleased to keep your word. Now I'll make you, ha, ha! yes. We, real intelligent people and people of action, differ from talkers, like many of your acquaintances, differ in that we don't allow ourselves to be taken in hand, but we do the taking, just as I took you, ha, ha! yes. (*Quietly to her.*) You boast of your freedom from biases, but there are some things that you would not want to make public. So, just know...

KATERINA MATVEYEVNA. Excuse me, excuse me...

VENEROVSKY. Go ahead...

KATERINA MATVEYEVNA. No, nothing. You are right, just let me think it through. (*Assumes her previous position.*) Please, leave me alone!... I will have my say later.

VENEROVSKY (*to* LYUBOCHKA). It's all over now with that lady. You stop it, too, sweetheart. I'm always condescending to people with weak characters and mental abilities, and that's quite natural, because I can see through all their petty strivings. But when they go against me, I make it a point to destroy that which hinders me. You would like to show that you have a will. That's praiseworthy and human, but the goal has to be sensible.

LYUBOCHKA (*heatedly*). You always think that only you are sensible. Katinka, you don't like me, but please, be honest, say something, stick up for me. I'm so sick of it, really sick of it! Why in the world did I leave them? At least if Dunyasha was with me! Katenka, what's wrong with you? (KATERINA MATVEYEVNA *doesn't answer.*)

KATERINA MATVEYEVNA. Lyubov, don't disturb me, I have to think things through. A great transformation is taking place inside of me. I feel it.

LYUBOCHKA. At least you tell me, Aleksey Pavlovich, would you harrass the woman you love? He finds faults with my relatives, he doesn't love me.

TVERDYNSKOY. Lyubov Ivanovna, I am, so to speak, a neophyte in love, and even an atheist therein.

LYUBOCHKA. You keep on joking, but for me it's not a joking matter. My God, why did I leave!

VENEROVSKY. Your way of speaking is quite unpleasant. But enough! I'm telling you for the last time: try to understand your desires, and to express them. That's very simple. I'm expressing myself clearly and sensibly, you also try to do the same.

LYUBOCHKA. Katinka always says this. Can you really express everything you feel? How can I say everything... You don't love me. Not for one minute did you think about me. Why do you keep on pestering me. I'm sick of it! You only praise yourself. Daddy would understand me.

VENEROVSKY. I told you that I'm above such talk, and your summons will not force me to enter the arena of sordid altercations. I will have the horses harnessed. Overseer!

SCENE 6

Enter OVERSEER.

VENEROVSKY. Hurry up, have the horses harnessed, I'll take your guys and pay double.

KATERINA MATVEYEVNA (*stands up and throws her head back*). Excuse me, Venerovsky! I have thought things through. Now I will tell you everything... (*Noise, a cry is heard behind the scene.*)

IVAN MIKHAILOVICH (*his voice*). Four horses for the carriage!

OVERSEER (*his voice*). None to be had, sir...

IVAN MIKHAILOVICH (*his voice*). You won't have a tooth left! Bandit! No, my friend, I've changed. They'll throw me in the slammer, but I'll knock out all your teeth. D'ya hear! Let me take a look. (*Enters.*)

SCENE 7

THE SAME *and* IVAN MIKHAILOVICH.

IVAN MIKHAILOVICH. Ah...ah...ah! My friends! Here they are! Caught them all in one swoop!...

TVERDYNSKOY. Not a bad little scandal brewing, let me tell you!

VENEROVSKY (*sits down on a chair opposite* IVAN MIKHAILOVICH *and stares at him impudently*). Here's a gentleman who ought to have his nose tweaked again.

KATERINA MATVEYEVNA (*remains in the same position*). I'm happy to see you, Ivan Mikhailovich.

LYUBOCHKA (*approaching her father*). Oh, Daddy...

PETRUSHA (*gets up from his place and gives his father a vacant look*). And now...hic!...everyone well understands...hic!...

IVAN MIKHAILOVICH (*to* LYUBA, *moving her aside*). Wait. We'll start with the strangers. (*To the* STUDENT, *takes him by the arm.*) My dear sir, please, come here!

TVERDYNSKOY. Do you really think that for your twenty roubles a month I have to kill myself?... It seems you yourself could understand...

IVAN MIKHAILOVICH. No, my little friend... Don't give me that old song. Did you obligate yourself to teach my son?

TVERDYNSKOY. You're not thinking of frightening me, are you?...only (*growing timid*) might makes right...isn't modern.

IVAN MIKHAILOVICH. "Modern!" We've heard that. And one who obligates himself to do something and for no reason doesn't carry it out, and, what's more, confuses a kid and takes him away from his parents' home, what would you call that man, my dear sir? You don't know? A fraud...

TVERDYNSKOY. You are impudent and I'll teach you, I won't allow anyone...

IVAN MIKHAILOVICH. Wha-at! (*Advances.*) Get out of here, out of my sight. If you were a little older, but as is you're pitiful, my dear sir...

TVERDYNSKOY. Naturally, that's all you can expect from ignoramuses and toothbusters. (*Retreats.*)

IVAN MIKHAILOVICH (*advances more resolutely*). Get out of here!

TVERDYNSKOY (*hurriedly grabbing his bundle, he walks to the doorway and shouts*). Contemptible reactionary!

SCENE 8

THE SAME *without* TVERDYNSKOY.

IVAN MIKHAILOVICH (*not paying further attention to* TVERDYNSKOY). Well, and now for the little darling! (*Going up to* PETRUSHA.) Sashka! (*Enter* FOOTMAN.) Did you take the rods?

FOOTMAN. They're in the carriage box, sir.

PETRUSHA. Individuality...in...di...

IVAN MIKHAILOVICH (*to the* FOOTMAN). Come here. Take this young man, pour a bucket of water over his head, do you hear? Then put him in the carriage...

PETRUSHA. The despotism...hic!...of parental power...individ...

IVAN MIKHAILOVICH (*turns* PETRUSHA *around and slaps the back of his head*). Enough of your talk! March! Sashka, take him down to the well, pour water on him, and keep him in the carriage.

PETRUSHA. What...what for? I can...

IVAN MIKHAILOVICH. Now!.....

FOOTMAN. So, Pyotr Ivanych... (*The* FOOTMAN *and* PETRUSHA *exit.*)

SCENE 9

THE SAME *without* PETRUSHA.

IVAN MIKHAILOVICH (*to* KATERINA MATVEYEVNA). Well, my cropped
emancipation, let me ask you: what, does your uncle keep a house of
ill repute, is that it? Huh?

KATERINA MATVEYEVNA. Ivan Mikhailovich! I share your convictions...

IVAN MIKHAILOVICH. No, young lady, no more of those words! I was a
fool, but I won't be again. What, did I manage your Lopukhovka
Estate on a whim? What, did I rob you, is that it? What, was I paid for
your upkeep? You received one hundred roubles a year from your village, but you write me...what's there to say, it stinks!

KATERINA MATVEYEVNA. You are absolutely right, Ivan Mikhailovich,
my conduct is inconsistent.

IVAN MIKHAILOVICH. What have Marya Vasilevna and I seen from you
besides contempt? And all of this was crowned with what? Your running away and this letter. (*Takes out the letter.*) I'm not your relative,
not your uncle. Just go wherever you want, with this pen-pusher.

KATERINA MATVEYEVNA. Yes, Uncle dear, yes, you're telling the truth.
Yes, Uncle dear, I acknowledge my error. I ask you to forget. I am an
unhappy woman, Uncle dear.

IVAN MIKHAILOVICH. You've deceived me enough, young lady... (*Looks
at* VENEROVSKY.) Enough!.....

VENEROVSKY. What are you looking at me for? I won't hide it from you,
Ivan Mikhailovich, I'm sick of your shouting. Go home—really, it'll be
more peaceful. There are no more children here, and no one to fright-
en.

IVAN MIKHAILOVICH. I'll go, my dear sir, when I've had my say.

VENEROVSKY. And what is it that you have to say, may I ask? I'll listen though I know everything you'll say, and I know there won't be anything new or witty...

IVAN MIKHAILOVICH. There's much I have to say to you, but I won't speak in the presence of your wife, sir, and my daughter. You consider it honorable to set a daughter against her father, but I, though an old-timer, know that if a wife doesn't respect her father, then she's not worth a damn, but if she doesn't respect her husband—it's even worse.

VENEROVSKY (to KATERINA MATVEYEVNA). It seems, this gentleman wishes to teach me about honor; that's rather comical.

KATERINA MATVEYEVNA. He is right, he is absolutely right, don't speak to me... (Turns away.)

VENEROVSKY (shrugs his shoulders). Overseer, have them bring the horses. And you, Ivan Mikhailovich, are amusing to me, just amusing.

IVAN MIKHAILOVICH (shouting). I told you enough, let's leave it. Go, and God be with you. Lyuba, I brought you Dunyasha, take her. We were hurt, very hurt...well, God be with you. You'll have children, then you'll understand. (Embraces her, she cries.)

VENEROVSKY. The comedy playing isn't bad, but it can get tiresome. Let's go, Lyubinka! Let's go and sit in that room. You can play the comedy by yourself.

LYUBOCHKA. I don't want to, Daddy! I won't go with him... Stay with me. (To VENEROVSKY.) Leave me alone.

IVAN MIKHAILOVICH. Have you lost your senses! Anatoly Dmitrievich, my dear friend, forgive me if I became excited. We'll remain...

VENEROVSKY (takes LYUBA by the arm). Lyuba, let's go, let your parent clown by himself, and with Katerina Matveyevna.

LYUBOCHKA. Daddy, what have I done! I'm afraid of him, I hate him. (LYUBA hides her face in her father's chest.)

IVAN MIKHAILOVICH. Have you lost your senses! What are you saying, Lyuba! You shouldn't!

KATERINA MATVEYEVNA (She steps forward solemnly, brushing her hair back). Now I will tell everything that is on my mind. Listen to me, Ivan Mikhailovich, listen to me, Venerovsky. Lyubov must leave this man. This man is a worthless and base individual.

VENEROVSKY (*tries to outshout her*). You're a stupid, undeveloped, and lewd woman. Shut up or I'll...

KATERINA MATVEYEVNA. No, Venerovsky, you won't frighten me! I'm a free person. You will not outshout me, I myself intend to tell it all. Venerovsky, you are a bastard, and it is not a woman who is telling you this but a free human being... He will ruin Lyuba if she remains with him, just as he ruined me and pushed me aside. Half an hour ago I considered myself above everyone in the world, but now I am an unhappy, pitiful, and contemptible creature.

VENEROVSKY. You're stupid and nothing more. And the way you're acting doesn't surprise me in the least; it proceeds directly from your stupidity. Lyubov Ivanovna, I'm asking you to come with me.

LYUBOCHKA. I won't go for anything. I'd rather die.

IVAN MIKHAILOVICH. My poor little girl, what have I done to you! Let's go. Good-bye, sir. Now I can tell you everything. You wanted to marry a fortune. You didn't love Lyubochka and didn't respect her. You only needed one thing: money, and you got it.[19] And in return for us giving you everything, even someone whose fingernail you're not worth, you made her unhappy, and spit into the face of people who wished you nothing but good. A nobody and arrogance! I'm completely to blame.

VENEROVSKY (*trying to outshout him, he grabs* LYUBA *by the arm*). I felt sorry for Lyuba, who was perishing in your hideous family, and I rescued her from your depravity. Lyuba, let's go! I won't let anyone ridicule me. I'll ridicule you. Let's go! (*Pulls her arm.*)

LYUBOCHKA. You're hurting me, I'm not going, I don't want to be your wife, I hate you...

KATERINA MATVEYEVNA. And this is a devotée to the new doctrine! Our doctrine!

IVAN MIKHAILOVICH (*advances*). Leave her alone. Now I'm telling you. (*Stands in front of* LYUBOCHKA; VENEROVSKY *wants to move forward.*) Another step—I'll bust you into little pieces!

VENEROVSKY. Ha ha! (*Backing off and slowly pulling a pistol out of his pocket.*) Did you think I didn't foresee this? Having dealings with people like you, I foresaw everything. I foresaw both insults and fights. Only we are people of action and won't allow ourselves to be ridiculed, ha, ha! Try to insult me now! (*Aims the pistol.*)

IVAN MIKHAILOVICH (*stops in front of him and shakes his head*). Fool! At whom are you shooting! Go ahead, shoot! Let's go, Lyuba! (*They exit.*)

SCENE 10

VENEROVSKY (*alone*). So, did you ridicule me?...ha-ha! No, we're not Tverdynskoys, you can't chase us away. Bekleshov was right, to deal with such people you have to renounce all principles. I was too honest with them. However, woman is free, and I don't recognize any rights over her. Well, here is the deed to her estate.[20] (*The* FOOTMAN *comes in for the shawl.*) Come here, take this document to your master. They won't understand why I'm returning this document, ha-ha! Yes, relations in this obdurate environment are still too savage and coarse! Or perhaps we have gone too far, we were born about one hundred years too early for there to be any sort of compromises between us.

The Nihilist

A Comedy in Three Acts

Glafira Fyodorovna
  an old lady
Fiona Andreyevna
  her companion, a hanger-on
  living in her home
Semyon [Senya, Simon] Ivanych
  Glafira Fyodorovna's son, a
  landowner, around 40
Marya [Masha] Dmitrievna
  his young wife
Lyuba
  her sister
Natalya [Natasha] Pavlovna
  Lyuba's girlfriend
Nikolinka [Nicolas]
  Semyon Ivanych's nephew, a
  high-school boy
Khrisanf Vasilevich
  a student, a nihilist, Nikolinka's
  teacher. [At times his name
  appears as Krisanf Vasilevich in
  the text of the play.]

  The action takes place in Semyon
  Ivanych's village.

ACT I

SCENE 1

GLAFIRA FYODOROVNA, FIONA ANDREYEVNA, *and* SEMYON IVANYCH *sitting at a table having tea.*

GLAFIRA FYODOROVNA. Senya, now you've invited a bunch of guests and I don't know what to do. It would be fine if they were decent people, but God only knows who they are. Yesterday they got into the pantry and rummaged through everything. They're up to something there. As it is, there are problems with servants nowadays. Ah, I've had it with these young people!

FIONA ANDREYEVNA. Ehh, my good man, these days you don't invite guests. You probably heard that in Zolotukhino, at the Zhitovskys, a coachman climbed through a window.

SEMYON IVANYCH. It's got nothing to do with a coachman, Glafira Fyodorovna. Why shouldn't young people have a good time, Momma? I'm only wondering, where have they all gone?

GLAFIRA FYODOROVNA. Yes, my dear, here you're thinking about their pleasure, but they've lost all respect for their elders. It's your name day, and so far no one has remembered it.

FIONA ANDREYEVNA. It's all because of new ways, my dear, there are genilists[1] all over the place. And you have to give them all food and drink.

SEMYON IVANYCH. Are there really that many? And Momma, why are you making such a fuss? We had to take my nephew in on his vacation, so he has his teacher with him, a student...

GLAFIRA FYODOROVNA. Oh, my goodness, you can't...

FIONA ANDREYEVNA. Saints alive!

SEMYON IVANYCH. Then, my sister-in-law, on break from the Institute, with her friend, a very nice girl.

GLAFIRA FYODOROVNA. These girlfriends, they'll be a handful.

FIONA ANDREYEVNA. They'll sure be, ma'am, they'll sure be.

SEMYON IVANYCH. What?

GLAFIRA FYODOROVNA. Nothing.

FIONA ANDREYEVNA. Nothing, my good man. Have some sugar, please.

SCENE 2

THE SAME, *and enter* MARYA DMITRIEVNA.

SEMYON IVANYCH. Ah, and here she is.

MARYA DMITRIEVNA (*in the doorway*). Look, don't forget. (*Goes up to everyone in turn and kisses her husband.*) Good morning, my dear, happy name day. Good morning, *maman*. Congratulations, it's your son's name day. Fiona Andreyevna, my respects.

GLAFIRA FYODOROVNA. It seems, today, *ma chère*, is a joyful day for us.

MARYA DMITRIEVNA. I know, I know very well. (*Kisses her husband.*)

SEMYON IVANYCH. Have you seen where they all are, where's Lyuba and all the young people?

MARYA DMITRIEVNA. I have... Ah no, I haven't.

GLAFIRA FYODOROVNA. How different it was in our time! When it was the name day of my Ivan Zakharych, rest his soul, you would get up at first light, look everything over, prepare various surprises, bouquets. Someone would learn a poem, my sister once learned a song on the clavichord...

FIONA ANDREYEVNA. And do you remember, my dear, how they put on a comedy—*The String.*

GLAFIRA FYODOROVNA. What string?

FIONA ANDREYEVNA. That's what it was called.

GLAFIRA FYODOROVNA. My darling would come in and everyone wished him happy name day. It was even touching to watch. It's not like that with you.

FIONA ANDREYEVNA. I can't think about it without tears. That's when a name day was really a name day, not like it is now. You really had a good cry seeing their love. (*Cries.*)

MARYA DMITRIEVNA. So that's the way it used to be, *maman*—is it worse now?

GLAFIRA FYODOROVNA. Yes, it's worse.

SCENE 3

THE SAME, NATALYA PAVLOVNA, LYUBA, *and the* STUDENT *run in.*

LYUBA. Good morning, Glafira Fyodorovna, I have the honor of congratulating you. It's your son's name day! Good morning, Semyon Ivanych, happy name day to you.

NATALYA PAVLOVNA (*curtsies affectedly*). Bonjour, madame, je vous félicité, et vous aussi, monsieur.

LYUBA (*cheerfully*). Why is it you're crying, Fiona Andreyevna! (*Walks off to the side.*)

KHRISANF VASILEVICH (*to* MASHA *quietly*). I got it, take a look.

MARYA DMITRIEVNA (*also quietly*). Good, very good.

SEMYON IVANYCH. What? (*A general silence.*)

KHRISANF VASILEVICH (*to* SEMYON IVANYCH). Since there is a custom of extending best wishes, my best wishes to you.

SEMYON IVANYCH (*to* MARYA DMITRIEVNA). Didn't you and Krisanf Vasilevich see each other already?

MARYA DMITRIEVNA (*confused*). No... Yes... No, we didn't, good morning.

KHRISANF VASILEVICH (*bowing*). Yes, we already did. (*To the* COMPANION.) Why is it you're bawling that way, Fiona Andreyevna? In these days of progress it has been proven that tears are only a function of the organism.

FIONA ANDREYEVNA. You and your urganism.[2] I can also call you bad names, I've seen better people than you. (*Turns away.*)

GLAFIRA FYODOROVNA. I'm very happy, *mes chers amis*, that you've come to visit my son. I'm just afraid that you might be bored with us old folks. Times are not the same now. *Et vous, ma chère, avez vous terminé vos études?* (*Addresses* NATALYA.)

NATALYA PAVLOVNA. *Non, madame, pas encore.* (LYUBA *pulls her dress from behind.*) I can't, they'll find out.

MARYA DMITRIEVNA. Oh, it's so hot here. (*Goes to the young people.*) For God's sake, be careful that he doesn't see! (*Silence.*)

GLAFIRA FYODOROVNA. Look how quickly your wife has become friendly with the guests.

SEMYON IVANYCH. What?

FIONA ANDREYEVNA. She's very sociable.

SCENE 4

THE SAME *and* NIKOLINKA.

NIKOLINKA (*runs in*). Congratulations to you, Glafira Fyodorovna, it's your son's name day. And to you best wishes, dear Uncle. (*Comically bows to* FIONA ANDREYEVNA; *walks over to the young people; they whisper among themselves and they all run off.*)
SEMYON IVANYCH. Masha, hey Masha!

SCENE 5

GLAFIRA FYODOROVNA, FIONA ANDREYEVNA, *and* SEMYON IVANYCH.

GLAFIRA FYODOROVNA. Yes, my dear, nowadays youth looks at things in its own way. I wouldn't say there's a great difference in your ages, but she could have paid more attention. It's sad, very sad.
FIONA ANDREYEVNA. They all ran off just like to a fire.
SEMYON IVANYCH (*angrily*). You shut up! (*Frightened,* FIONA ANDREYEVNA *stands up.*)
GLAFIRA FYODOROVNA. Oh, my dear, how you shout! Your wife ran off with that student instead of being with her husband, but is she to blame that you're jealous of her over that kid!
SEMYON IVANYCH (*standing up*). Oh, *maman*, the things you say! Why! Would I really sink so low as to be jealous? The very word is repugnant to me. (*He bangs his fist on the table angrily.*) And let me tell you that if you want to make me quarrel with my wife...
GLAFIRA FYODOROVNA. Oh, my dear boy, God help you, don't shout at me. You invited God knows who, and I'm to blame. Let's go, Fiona Andreyevna, I see we're not needed.
FIONA ANDREYEVNA. Not needed, my dear, not needed. (*They exit.*)

SCENE 6

SEMYON IVANYCH (*alone*). Jealous—not jealous, that's nonsense. But it's strange, really strange. What's this winking, whispering among themselves—she ran off... And all of the girls are so happy with this bony Krisanf, whatever his name. It's all an example. The girls flirt and she goes along with them. Oh, sure, that's just fine for girls! Incomprehensible! Nevertheless, why the secret smiles, winks? Oh, how unpleasant! No, it's horrible... Yes, horrible. Oh, women! (*He exits.*)

ACT II

SCENE 1

MARYA DMITRIEVNA, LYUBA, NATALYA PAVLOVNA, *and* NIKOLINKA *are looking over a transparency. The room is in disorder, with paper, starch, and costumes.*

MARYA DMITRIEVNA. Khrisanf has done great, just great. God sent us this Khrisanf.

NATALYA PAVLOVNA (*laughs*). Oh, Marya Dmitrievna, how sick I am of him! He took it into his head to court me, talks about some sort of rational love. He's so repulsive!

LYUBA. It's not true, Masha, she's very happy. She herself flirts with him.

NATALYA PAVLOVNA. Me? What nonsense! No, Marya Dmitrievna, it was she who was flirting with him. She kept on talking about emancipation.

LYUBA. No, it was you.

NATALYA PAVLOVNA (*hurt*). I'm sorry, it was not me.

LYUBA. Yes it was!

NATALYA PAVLOVNA (*in the same tone*). Please, it wasn't me.

LYUBA. Yes it was.

MARYA DMITRIEVNA. Enough, enough of your arguing. It's time to get down to business. We haven't even finished the S.[3]

LYUBA. No, Masha, I can't; we have to call Khrisanf Vasilevich.

NATALYA PAVLOVNA. *Nicolas*, run and get him. (NIKOLINKA *runs off.*)

SCENE 2

THE SAME, *without* NIKOLINKA.

NATALYA PAVLOVNA (*comes up to* MASHA, *very animated*). Marya Dmitrievna, when he works, he takes off his frock coat. Let him do it. You'll see what kind of print shirt he has.

SCENE 3

THE SAME, *enter the* STUDENT *with* NIKOLINKA.

MARYA DMITRIEVNA. Is the poem ready?

LYUBA. Smear soot on the *transparent*, otherwise I'll get my hands dirty.

NATALYA PAVLOVNA. What about the lanterns?

KHRISANF VASILEVICH (*stops in the doorway*). Here it is, the equality of women. God alone can be omnipresent, but I can't be everywhere. No, I told you, Natalya Pavlovna, that our women are still far from understanding rational love.

LYUBA. It's got nothing to do with love, smear the soot.

MARYA DMITRIEVNA. Take off your frock coat.

NATALYA PAVLOVNA. Glue the lanterns.

KHRISANF VASILEVICH. If you won't mind. (*Takes off his frock coat.*)

MARYA DMITRIEVNA. Please do. Nikolinka, go to the porch; if someone comes by, run in and tell us.

NIKOLINKA. You can relax, I won't let a soul slip by. (*Runs off.*)

THE SAME, *without* NIKOLINKA. *All turn their attention to the* STU-DENT'*s shirt.*

NATALYA PAVLOVNA (*mockingly*). Lilac!

MARYA DMITRIEVNA (*also mockingly*). Dirty!

LYUBA. With little blue flowers!

KHRISANF VASILEVICH. What? What?

LYUBA. Nothing, I'm only saying that little blue flowers will look very good on the lantern.

KHRISANF VASILEVICH. I did ask for your cooperation, ladies.

NATALYA PAVLOVNA. All right, I'll glue. (*She glues a star on his shirt.*)

LYUBA (*painting the collar of his shirt*). And I'll paint.

MARYA DMITRIEVNA. Well, what about the poem?

KHRISANF VASILEVICH. Give me a moment for inspiration, Marya Dmitrievna. (*He runs his hand over his hair and smears his forehead with soot.*)

NATALYA PAVLOVNA AND LYUBA (*together*). More, more inspiration!

KHRISANF VASILEVICH (*not noticing it, he dirties his face again*). All right. (*Walks off to the side and strikes a pose.*) "Best wishes on your name day…" No, it's no good…

NIKOLINKA (*runs in*). He's coming, he's coming!

MARYA DMITRIEVNA. Who's coming?

NIKOLINKA. Nikolai the cook.

LYUBA. Oh, you idiot!

MARYA DMITRIEVNA. The cook doesn't matter, only if it's one of our own people coming…

KHRISANF VASILEVICH. Excuse me, excuse me, ladies. You've smeared me and glued things to me. Twice you've glued things to me.

NATALYA PAVLOVNA. But there's still no poem.

MARYA DMITRIEVNA. Well, do what you want with your inspiration, and we'll go on gluing.

KHRISANF VASILEVICH (*aside*). "Best wishes on your name day…" No, it's no good. "We bring greetings…" (*Thinks.*) I'll take one that's done… Here you go, Marya Dmitrievna, it's ready. (*Recites.*)

Though the Graces with bouquets
Are not in vogue nowadays,
I'm a conservative through and through,
And my thoughts are only of you!

Do you want more?

MARYA DMITRIEVNA. Enough. Great, very good. Dressed as the three Graces, we'll bring him the monogram, and I'll sing the verses. I'm very grateful to you, Khrisanf Vasilevich. (*Squeezes the* STUDENT's *hand. At that moment the window opens and* SEMYON IVANYCH's *head appears. Frightened, meanwhile the girls cover the lanterns.*) Oh, Semyon Ivanych, don't come here, don't come!

SEMYON IVANYCH (*looks with horror at his wife*). Ah, you're all here. I'm very happy that you're having a good time. All right, all right, I'll leave.

NATALYA PAVLOVNA. My God, he saw everything!

LYUBA. No he didn't, he didn't!

MARYA DMITRIEVNA. Where's that damned Nikolinka? Lyuba, drag him over here. (NIKOLINKA *collides with* LYUBA *who is running toward him.*)

NIKOLINKA (*running in*). He's coming, he himself is coming.

MARYA DMITRIEVNA. What have you done?

LYUBA. Where were you?

NATALYA PAVLOVNA. Oh, everything's ruined!

KHRISANF VASILEVICH. Unfaithful servant, I made you a lookout in my orchard, and you slept. (*Everyone plays rough with* NIKOLINKA.)

LYUBA. I'll tickle you to death.

NATALYA PAVLOVNA. I'll smear you with soot.

NIKOLINKA (*struggling*). Let me go, let me go!

SCENE 5

THE SAME, FIONA ANDREYEVNA.

FIONA ANDREYEVNA (*horrified*). My God, they've choked the child. Kuzma! People! Someone!

KHRISANF VASILEVICH. Madam, as pleasant as your company is for us, at the moment we'd shed no tears if we had to do without it.

FIONA ANDREYEVNA. Oh, you!

LYUBA. Go! Go away! (*Slams the door.*)

FIONA ANDREYEVNA (*complaining and showing her dress*). It's crepe-Rachel! My benefactress gave it to me!

MARYA DMITRIEVNA. Oh, you and your benefactress!

FIONA ANDREYEVNA (*looks in from the door*). Oh, what horrors, the student is got up like the devil! I'll go and tell everything. (*Exits.*)

MARYA DMITRIEVNA. Go away! Nikolinka, go on the lookout, and we'll get to work.

KHRISANF VASILEVICH. Why in the world did she say the student was got up like the devil? Let me take a look. (*Looks into the mirror and angrily tears off a piece of paper.*) How stupid. Nothing witty about it. I humbly thank you, Natalya Pavlovna, this is all your witticism. (*Puts on his frock coat.*)

LYUBA. It wasn't Natasha at all, it got stuck by itself.

NATALYA PAVLOVNA AND MARYA DMITRIEVNA. By itself, by itself.

KHRISANF VASILEVICH. What underdevelopment!

MARYA DMITRIEVNA. Oh, that's enough, Khrisanf Vasilevich. Can't you take a joke! But I have to go so's not to get caught.

NIKOLINKA (*runs in*). She's coming, she herself is coming, as big as day! (*They run senselessly around the table shouting: My God!*)

MARYA DMITRIEVNA. Enough of that, take everything out of here, hide! (*All run off except* MARYA DMITRIEVNA *and* KHRISANF VASILEVICH.)

SCENE 6

MARYA DMITRIEVNA, KHRISANF VASILEVICH, *and* GLAFIRA FYODOROVNA.

GLAFIRA FYODOROVNA. Cute, very cute. *Simon*! Poor *Simon*! You didn't even have pity on my gray hair. And for whom? Look at this smearer!

KHRISANF VASILEVICH (*with dignity*). What right do you have?

MARYA DMITRIEVNA. Later, *maman*, I'll explain everything later. Let's go, Khrisanf Vasilevich. (*Takes the* STUDENT *away.*)

SCENE 7

GLAFIRA FYODOROVNA *alone, then* FIONA ANDREYEVNA.

GLAFIRA FYODOROVNA (*alone*). You've no shame, no conscience! That's right, madam! Just took her sweetheart's arm and left. My God! No, I can't bear this. Fiona Andreyevna!

FIONA ANDREYEVNA (*runs in*). My benefactress!

ACT III

SCENE 1

GLAFIRA FYODOROVNA *and* FIONA ANDREYEVNA *lay out cards.*

FIONA ANDREYEVNA. And she hears an unusual noise, she looks and looks, and there are rings under her icons, all rings...

GLAFIRA FYODOROVNA. What kind of rings?

FIONA ANDREYEVNA. Now that, my dear, was God's sign to her... Well, so off she goes to the elder, comes to his cell, looks, and there's a pig sitting there...and a demon above it. She went and passed out like a light. Luckily a novice came in, sprinkled her, and said: that's nothing, he's our holy fool! Sometimes he turns himself into God knows what.

GLAFIRA FYODOROVNA (*hands her the cards*). Shuffle the cards.

FIONA ANDREYEVNA. As you wish, my dear. So, my lady, that elder gave her some advice: Go, he says, to the Solovki monks.[4]

GLAFIRA FYODOROVNA. Where?

FIONA ANDREYEVNA. To the Solovki monks, my dear. Well, so off she goes—goes and goes, and all the time he's before her eyes.

GLAFIRA FYODOROVNA. Who?

FIONA ANDREYEVNA. The demon, of course. And all of a sudden her leg begins to hurt, there's a lump.

GLAFIRA FYODOROVNA. What?

FIONA ANDREYEVNA. A lump, my dear, a real big one. What can she do? She stopped at an old woman's place, and the elder, Father Anfilogy, told her: take care, never sleep on your right side because he's there...

GLAFIRA FYODOROVNA. Now why, my dear woman, are you telling this in such a mixed up way? Who's there?

FIONA ANDREYEVNA. He, my dear. Who else—Father Anfilogy says: at the birth of each man, it says in the Scriptures...

GLAFIRA FYODOROVNA. Well, enough of that. I have other things on my mind. Where's our Senya? Poor *Simon*! I can't even think about it. There he is, let's go. (*They exit.*)

SCENE 2

SEMYON IVANYCH *alone, then* NATALYA PAVLOVNA.

SEMYON IVANYCH (*enters, gloomy*). No, I can't take this any longer. Momma summoned me and told me in plain words that she herself saw my wife speaking secretly with that gentleman. She says... But it's terrible what she says and thinks... Let's assume that it's nonsense, but how could she bring herself to give cause for thinking that about her! But I have to make up my mind. I can't leave it like this. I'll go to her and clear things up. Masha, Masha, how I loved you! But this gentleman, well this gentleman now, he won't get off easy—no, he won't! (*Takes hold of a club.*)

SCENE 3

NATALYA PAVLOVNA (*enters*). It seems you're sad, Semyon Ivanych, are you?

SEMYON IVANYCH. Me? No, I'm fine.

NATALYA PAVLOVNA. What's that horrible stick? What's it for?

SEMYON IVANYCH. It's just... (*He is silent.*) Natalya Pavlovna, what would you do if you loved a person with all your heart, and that person had no regrets about insulting you, striking you in your most sensitive spot?

NATALYA PAVLOVNA. I can't imagine, I haven't experienced it.

SEMYON IVANYCH (*takes up the stick*). I know what to do. (*Makes a*

threatening gesture with the club.) No, nothing. Good-bye. (NATALYA
PAVLOVNA *exits.*) Oh, no... Where's Masha? I'll go and resolve everything, without fail I'll do it! (*Goes.*)

MARYA DMITRIEVNA (*from behind the door*). Senya, is that you? Go out
for a moment, will you please.

SEMYON IVANYCH (*aside*). She doesn't even want to hide it! I don't understand.

SCENE 4

KHRISANF VASILEVICH (*takes the candles, moves away the table and
chairs*). You're being asked to go out for a moment.

SEMYON IVANYCH (*takes up the stick*). Stop, wait!

KHRISANF VASILEVICH. No time now, later. (*Exits, carrying away the candles.*)

SCENE 5

LYUBA (*runs up to the door*). Glafira Fyodorovna, dear, come quickly!
What we have going on, it's lovely! Come! (*Runs off.*)

SCENE 6

GLAFIRA FYODOROVNA, FIONA ANDREYEVNA, *and* SEMYON IVANYCH,
then all the others.

GLAFIRA FYODOROVNA. What is it now? The end of the world?

FIONA ANDREYEVNA. My dear, at least recite a prayer in the dark.

SEMYON IVANYCH. No, I can't bear it, either I or... They've gone mad, I
don't understand a thing!

SCENE 7

They all enter in costumes with the transparency.

MARYA DMITRIEVNA (*sings the verses*).

Though the Graces with bouquets
Are not in vogue nowadays,
I'm a conservative through and through,
And my thoughts are only of you.

(FIONA ANDREYEVNA, GLAFIRA FYODOROVNA, *and* SEMYON IVANYCH
cry.)

SEMYON IVANYCH. Oh, I am a fool! And I thought...

MARYA DMITRIEVNA. What did you think?

SEMYON IVANYCH. No, I won't say.

MARYA DMITRIEVNA. Now you see.

GLAFIRA FYODOROVNA. *Charmant*, how sweet! Children, give me a hug.

FIONA ANDREYEVNA. There's a nihilist, got us in the heart!

KHRISANF VASILEVICH. Now then my splendid lady, Fiona Andreyevna,
let's me and you also conclude a reconciliation.

Dramatization of the Legend about Aggeus

The origin of the name Aggeus is uncertain (Greek?). The legend itself is based on *The Tale of Emperor Jovinian* (in *Gesta Romanorum*), which in Russia also existed as a separate tale that was reworked and known as *The Tale of Emperor Aggeus and How He Was Afflicted by Pride.*

Servants (3)
House Servant
Drivers (3)
Bandits (2)
Young Bandit
Young Shepherd
Old Shepherd
Old Man
Peasant
Cottage Owner
Peasant Woman
Blind Beggar
Armless Beggar
Yardman
Huntsman
Coachman
Master (in last scene, double of the real Master, Fadey)

Tolstoy did not provide a list of the dramatis personae for this play.
It has been prepared by the translator for the convenience of the reader.

VIGNETTE I

At the doors of a church. SERVANTS *stand with sedan chairs waiting for their* MASTER *and his* WIFE.

SCENE 1

FIRST, SECOND *and* THIRD SERVANT.

FIRST SERVANT. Now he's taken it into his head to go to church.

SECOND SERVANT. It's about time, I've been livin' in his home for twenty years—hasn't been once.

FIRST SERVANT. Probably wants to repent.

THIRD SERVANT. And it's about time too. He's caused more than a couple of tears to flow. He's beaten Pyotr to a pulp. Took away Semyon's wife, Fyodor's daughter. People are sufferin', they curse 'im, but he, he don't care, has a good time. Drinks from mornin' to night, goofs off, goes huntin'. And he don't ever give a coin to a beggar, won't let 'em near his place. Only why does God put up with his sins?

SECOND SERVANT. Repent? Fat chance! That's not like 'im. Just wait, he'll even pull a stunt in church. (*Thunder and lightening.*) My God, what's goin' on? There's a clear sky and it's thunderin'.

SCENE 2

A HOUSE SERVANT *runs out of the church.*

HOUSE SERVANT. That's our master for yuh! Oh boy, the thing he did! (*They surround the* HOUSE SERVANT.)

FIRST, SECOND, AND THIRD SERVANTS. What? What? Talk straight.

HOUSE SERVANT. So listen! He walked into church in the middle of the service, hat on, stood right in the middle lookin' around. The deacon came out to read the Gospel. He read up to the place where it says: "But woe unto you that are rich! for ye have received your consolation. Woe unto you that are full! for ye shall hunger. Woe unto you that laugh now! for ye shall mourn and weep."[1] Then the master yelled out: "You're full of crap, gimme the book." He grabbed it and started to tear it. As soon as he gave a tear, it began to thunder. So out I ran.

SCENE 3

The MASTER *comes out followed by the others.*

MASTER. Look at that, he reads that the poor'll be blessed and the rich become poor. How's that possible? How will I become poor when I own a hundred villages, and everything around here's mine? Lies are written in the book, and you shouldn't read lies. So I tore out these pages and I'll put them in my pocket. No more reading. (*Thunder and lightening.*) I'm not afraid. Reading lies! And just as I've lived rich, so'll I live all my life, I won't become poor. (*To the people.*) What are you so scared of? You were told to get ready for the drive. Get going! I'll just have dinner at home and be right out. I want you all waiting in the woods. (*Gets into the sedan chair and is carried off. Thunder.*)
MASTER. Thunder away, away, I'm not afraid.

VIGNETTE II

A woods. Horns blow.

SCENE 1

Two DRIVERS.

FIRST DRIVER. Did'ya see the master?
SECOND DRIVER. I only saw 'im when he jumped down from his horse.
FIRST DRIVER. But how come he let the horse go?
SECOND DRIVER. He shot a deer while ridin' and it dropped. He was happy, jumped down and went to finish it off. But the deer jumped up

and took off. He went after it on foot. And now his horse runs away. Off we go to catch it. But it lifts its tail and heads for home. (*Enter* THIRD DRIVER.)

THIRD DRIVER. What are yuh doin' here?

FIRST AND SECOND DRIVER. We're lookin' for the master.

THIRD DRIVER. Yuh're lookin' for nothin'. He's already home.

FIRST DRIVER. What d'ya mean? What about the horse?

THIRD DRIVER. We caught it and brought it to 'im. He got on and left.

SECOND DRIVER. No shit?

THIRD DRIVER. Saw it myself. I held the stirrup when he got on. (*They exit.*)

SCENE 2

A deer runs by and stops behind a bush. The MASTER *runs in, hatless with knife in hand.*

MASTER. Where is it? Where is it? It was just here. Those damn bastards! They all fell behind, and they let the horse go. Just wait till I get back— I'll thrash every last one of 'em. (*The deer appears, the* MASTER *runs after it. Both disappear and appear again. The deer lets him approach, then runs off. If possible have water across which the deer swims followed by the* MASTER *without his clothes.*)

VIGNETTE III

A dark woods.

SCENE 1

MASTER (*if there is a river, naked, if not, in his clothes, but ragged, without his gun, horn, knife, and hat*). Hey, anyone! You devils, scoundrels, demons, I'll flog you to death! Hello-oo! Hello... No, no answer. Just let me get to you. You'll pay me for everything, you devil's spawn!

Scattered all over the place, left me alone. Just wait! Hello-oo!... (*Listens.*) No one. (*Lies down.*) There's a deer for you, it got me! I'll even have to spend the night here. Just wait, you devils. Boy will I flog you, first one, then another, I'll go through the whole lot. Then I'll begin all over again. You'll remember. Hello-oo! No one. (*Stands up.*) But you better get going: maybe you'll come across some people or a clearing. Them there wolves can get you here. Hello-oo! My throat's even dry. Just wait, I'll make your backs good and wet. Hello-oo! (*Exits.*)

SCENE 2

Enter BANDITS *with guns and sacks; they make camp and start a fire.*

FIRST BANDIT. People were always afraid of us bandits, and now it's come to us bein' afraid of people. The master's damn hunt really hurt us. We're holed up now in the furthest corner of the woods, and even here they've gotten to us.

SECOND BANDIT. Yeah, pal, we haven't robbed no one all day, only been runnin' away ourselves. Gotta get out on the road earlier tomorrow...to get some loot.

FIRST BANDIT. Life would be pretty good. Just one thing—there's no peace.

YOUNG BANDIT. Why are yuh so afraid of the master?

FIRST BANDIT. Why are we afraid? What an idiot. Why shouldn't we be afraid? He's no peasant nor no merchant: just the two of us could take care of those. But the master don't come out unless there's about a hundred riders with guns and knives followin' 'im, and about two hundred foot sloggers with clubs. That guy runs into us, there'll be nothin' but a blot left.

SECOND BANDIT. That's why yuh clear out right now.

FIRST BANDIT. What else. Yuh don't sue the rich, yuh don't fight the strong. And these woods here are all his. And the villages around here are his. He's a big man, he's got big power. He's a bandit just like us, only does it in a different way.

MASTER (*his cries are heard behind the scene*). Hello-oo!... You devils!...
I'll spill your guts! Hello-oo!

SCENE 3

The BANDITS *listen.*

YOUNG BANDIT (*jumps up*). A goblin! A goblin! He's yellin'.

FIRST BANDIT. Some goblin. Let's see what kind! (*The* MASTER *approaches.*)

SECOND BANDIT. And yuh got scared! It's no goblin. Just someone who's
got lost. Probably drunk. Hey, you, dude!

MASTER (*sees the people*). So that's where you are, you bandits! Found
yourself a spot, made a fire. And you dumped your master. Just you
wait, I'll show you! (*He rushes them, starts to fight.*)

FIRST BANDIT (*stands up, takes him by the collar*). Hey, hero. There's a
fighter! Take it easy! (*Grabs him by the arms.*)

MASTER. You bastards, dummies, you devils! I'll show you!

FIRST BANDIT. Hey guys, he's some sort of nut. Hand me the belt.

MASTER. What's the matter with you, don't you know your master? I'll
flay your hide, and then hang you by the legs.

FIRST BANDIT (*twists his arms back*). Come on, Sidorka, pull it tighter. I'll
lay a few warm ones on this master so's he forgets his mastery. (*Takes a
whip.*) Look at 'im, says he's the master.

YOUNG BANDIT. Really looks like the master, what's to say.

MASTER. I'll hang you!

FIRST BANDIT (*whips him*). One! Let's see you jump, Master.

MASTER. Ah, ah!

FIRST BANDIT. How's about another warm one. Is this how yuh'll whip us,
or is there another way?

MASTER. Ah, ah! Really, I am the master. Honest to God.

FIRST BANDIT. Yeah, I do believe yuh. That's exactly why I'm whippin'
yuh. (*Laughs.*) Just let me take yur clothes off, then we can better see
yur mastery. (*They whip him and tie him to a tree.*)

VIGNETTE IV

SCENE 1

Morning. The woods. The MASTER, *naked, is tied to a tree. He groans.*

MASTER. Oh, oh, oh! My hands are numb. Oh! Just wait, I'll get even for everything. I'll flog you with iron rods. Oh, my back! They've beat it raw. Well, you'll pay for it! I'll show you! Yes, I'll get to you. Oh, oh! I'm all dry in the mouth. I'll shut you away in cellars. I'll starve you to death.

SCENE 2

SHEPHERDS. *An old and young one.*

YOUNG SHEPHERD. Uncle, that's a man there tied up. Come, take a look.

OLD SHEPHERD. Now that there's a sin. Probably bandits robbed 'im and tied 'im up.

MASTER (*having seen them*). What are you standing there for, you idiots. Can't you see, untie me, quickly.

OLD SHEPHERD. Ah, people have no fear of God. How they've savaged the man. (*He approaches, wants to untie him.*) Look at those knots! Vanka, hand me your knife.

MASTER. Why're you screwing around, quicker! Oh-h-h!!

OLD SHEPHERD (*after untying and cutting him loose*). There now, buddy, yuh've straightened out. D'ya want some water? Vanka, get some water and bread.

YOUNG SHEPHERD (*brings some water and bread*). Here, buddy, have some.

MASTER (*lies down and groans*). Ah, bandits, the things they do. Well, now you won't slip out of my hands.

YOUNG SHEPHERD. Uncle, he's threatenin' someone.

OLD SHEPHERD. Leave 'im be. He's out of his head, let 'im come to himself. We really should cover 'im. (*Takes off his old overcoat, wants to put it over him.*) Here yuh are, poor guy, at least cover yuhself.

MASTER (*looks around and pushes the coat away*). What's the matter with you? Are you crazy or what?—putting a sackcloth on me. Do you know who I am? I'm your master. Take off your waistcoat and hat right now, clean 'em off good and put 'em on me. I'll wear 'em, let it be so. And take me to my house, to the master's house.

OLD SHEPHERD. He must be out of his head, says he's the master, but I saw the master myself ridin' home yesterday. (*To the* MASTER.) Enough, enough, put on what yuh're given, and go to the village. Yuh can lie down there.

MASTER (*jumps up*). So you're the same as those others. Just wait—you'll get yours too. Just how dare you talk in front of the master with your hat on! (*Knocks off his hat.*) Give me the waistcoat. (*Grabs him.*)

OLD SHEPHERD (*picks up his hat, pushes the* MASTER *away and walks off*). Let's go, Vanka, he's a real nut.

YOUNG SHEPHERD. We've untied yuh from the tree, fed yuh, Uncle gave yuh his overcoat, and yuh're still carryin' on. Cut it out, or else I'll slug yuh. (*Picks up his whip and pushes him. The* MASTER *falls. The* SHEPHERDS *exit. The* MASTER *lies on the ground groaning.*)

SCENE 3

PEASANTS *come.*

PEASANT. Look, there's a man there!

MASTER. Hey, folks, run quickly to the master's house and say that the master has been found. And have them send a carriage and servants for me here, and let me have a cottage, I'll rest.

OLD MAN. What are yuh talkin' about?

MASTER. What am I talking about? I'm your master.

OLD MAN. What master? The master's livin' at home in his chambers and not runnin' around barefoot.

MASTER. You idiots! I got lost chasing a deer, I'm the master. They're looking for me.

OLD MAN. Enough of yur bullshittin'. The master rode by yesterday, we saw 'im ourselves. And today he sent his foreman. He's at home.

MASTER. You're bullshitting, you bandits! I'll show you!

OLD MAN. Enough, young fellow. They say the shepherds gave yuh a beat-in' already. What, it's not enough for yuh, want some more? You cut it out. Get on yur way.

MASTER. They don't believe me. Oh, you bandits, I'll get to you. Now listen to me. You don't believe I'm your master? Well then, give me some paper, a pen, I'll write a letter to the master's wife. She'll know—because I'll write something that only she and I know about.

OLD MAN. Enough talk, get lost!

PEASANT. Why, Uncle, let 'im write, we can take it down to the village. (*They lift up the* MASTER *and take him away.*)

VIGNETTE V

In the PEASANT'*s cottage. The* MASTER. *A* PEASANT WOMAN.

MASTER. I'm all tired out. What's taking them so long, it's time I got an answer. They're in no rush, they don't know. My wife'll be really happy. (*Looks out of the window.*) Here he comes. (*Enter the* MESSENGER.)

MASTER. Well, where's the carriage, where are my people?

OLD MAN. Well, pal, yuh're a real joker!

MASTER. What, what? How dare you speak that way!

PEASANT. I just dare because the master ordered yuh...

MASTER. What master?

PEASANT. That one, the real one, not like you. He ordered yuh, master, whipped out of here, so's there'd be neither hide nor hair of yuh.

MASTER. My God, what is this? What about my wife?

PEASANT. I don't know about yur wife, if yuh have one, but the master's wife said: "That there could be such fakers. Chase 'im away."

MASTER. My God, my God, what'll become of me? (*Weeps.*)

COTTAGE OWNER. Strange business! So, pal, yur stunt didn't work, get goin', let God be with yuh.

VIGNETTE VI

SCENE 1

In the yard. The MASTER *is shoveling manure along with a* PEASANT
WOMAN.

PEASANT WOMAN. There's a cripple, don't even know how to hold a
   pitchfork. (*Taking away the pitchfork.*) Give it here, I'll do it myself, a
   real master.
MASTER. I would be happy to, but I don't know how.
PEASANT WOMAN. Yuh know how to eat bread.
MASTER. Oh, what a life. I'd better off dead.
PEASANT WOMAN. At least pull. (*He hitches himself, pulls, and falls.*)
PEASANT WOMAN. He can't even do that. I'm tired of yuh.

SCENE 2

MASTER. Well, you pretty thing.
PEASANT WOMAN. You're a nasty one! (*The* COTTAGE OWNER *comes.*)
PEASANT WOMAN. Here yuh gave me this dummy, work he don't know
   how, just looks to do nasty things.
COTTAGE OWNER. What? Yuh makin' up to my woman? I'll make up to
   yuh. Get out of here! Yuh're some master! (*Throws him out.*)

VIGNETTE VII

SCENE 1

A large village. The MASTER *enters barefoot, without a hat, in just a torn
   overcoat, and lies down at the edge of the road.*
MASTER. It's good that I got on the road. Now I can make my way home.

They'll recognize me there. So far no matter how many times I said I'm the master, no one believes me. They just curse me. If I won't say it, they'll give me something. If I do, they'll chase me away. And today I haven't eaten anything. So I won't say it. (*Goes up to a cottage, knocks.*) Give me something to eat. (*The window opens.*)

PEASANT WOMAN. There are a lot of yuh hangin' around! Look at yuh, such a strong guy beggin'—yuh should work.

MASTER. I'm not a beggar, I'm the master.

PEASANT WOMAN. If you're the master, there's no reason to knock on the window! (*Slams the window.*)

SCENE 2

Two BEGGARS *come—one blind, one armless, they go up to the window.*

BLIND AND ARMLESS BEGGARS. For Christ's sake!

PEASANT WOMAN (*opens the window and gives them bread*). Here yuh are, for Christ's sake. (*The* BEGGARS *sit down and eat.*)

MASTER (*goes up to them*). Give me something to eat.

BLIND BEGGAR. Why don't yuh beg yourself?

MASTER. I did—they didn't give.

ARMLESS BEGGAR. Well, have some. (*Gives him some bread, they eat.*) So who are yuh, where yuh from?

MASTER. I don't want to say anymore. As soon as I say who I am, everyone curses and beats me. They don't believe me. I don't know how to work, but I want to eat. Please have pity on me, take me with you.

ARMLESS BEGGAR. Why not, let's take 'im! Let 'im carry the sack.

BLIND BEGGAR. Let's go. (*The* BEGGARS *get up and exit with the* MASTER.)

VIGNETTE VIII

The MASTER's *house. The* SERVANTS *are dressed up. They play balalaikas and dance. The* BEGGARS *and the* MASTER *enter through the gates singing verses about Lazarus.*[2]

YARDMAN. My orders are to keep everyone out, beat it!

HUNTSMAN. I'll turn the dogs loose. Phew! Sic 'em! (*The dogs rush out, the* MASTER *goes to the door.*)

COACHMAN. There's a smart aleck! Let 'em bite your shins, then yuh'll know. Sic 'im!

MASTER. Oh, oh!...

YARDMAN (*takes him by the collar and drags him to the gate*). Beat it while yuh're still in one piece.

MASTER. I'm here. (*The other* MASTER *looks out of the window. The* MASTER *becomes quiet and looks.*)

BEGGAR MASTER. My God! I'm at home. There's another me in the window, what's going on?

MASTER IN THE WINDOW. Leave 'em, leave the beggars alone. This is for them. (*Throws a handful of silver.*) Let the blind ones sing, and then feed 'em. (*The* BEGGARS *sing about Lazarus.*)

MASTER IN THE WINDOW. Bring the one carrying the sack into my chambers.

VIGNETTE IX

The royal chamber. The MASTER, *as a beggar, is dining alone and is served by* SERVANTS.

MASTER. What does this mean? There was another me at the window, with a serene and kindly look. And he stood up for me and had me received here separately. My life is finished. No one will ever, ever recognize me. Evidently, I am to perish in need. What's this? (*A light appears and from the light a* VOICE.)

VOICE. Do you, Master Fadey, know a powerful, rich, and proud master

who did not believe the word of the Gospel, and said a rich man cannot become poor? Have you now learned what the riches of this world
are for, and how you can rely on them? Do you understand that this
was a vision, and why you had this vision? Have you repented of your
pride?

MASTER. I have repented, and shall not live as I did before.

VOICE. Then be you a master again, and merit your pride. (*The* MASTER
changes clothes. His WIFE *enters and embraces him, the* SERVANTS
bow.)

VIGNETTE X

A large, sumptuous table. BEGGARS *sit at the table, served by the* MAS-
TER *and his* WIFE.

The First Moonshiner

or How the Demon Earned His Bread

A Comedy

Peasant

Demon (also Peasants' Demon, Farmhand Demon, Potap)

Dudes' Demon

Chief (demon)

Clerk (demon)

Lawyers' Demon

Neighbor

Wife (Peasant's, Marya)

Old Man

Old Woman

Grandfather

Grandmother

Old Men (4—in addition to Old Man. Also, some have names: Uncle Mikhaila, Uncle Karp, Ivan Fedotych)

Girls

Boys

Tolstoy did not provide a list of the dramatis personae for this play.
It has been prepared by the translator for the convenience of the reader.

ACT I

SCENE 1

PEASANT (*plowing, looks up*). Noon already, time to quit. Go on, get movin'! Yuh've had it, eh old girl? I'll make one more pass, do a last furrow, and then lunch. Luckily I thought of takin' a chunk of bread along. I won't go home. Just eat by the well, take a snooze while Brownie munches on some grass. Then, with God's help, back to work. I'll finish up early, God willin'.

SCENE 2

A DEMON *runs to a bush.*

DEMON. Look here, such a good one! Keeps on bringin' up God! Just you wait, yuh'll bring up the devil too. I'll take away his chunk of bread. He'll realize it's gone and begin lookin' for it. He'll want to eat, he'll curse and bring up the devil. (*Takes the chunk of bread, goes off and sits down behind the bush, watching what the* PEASANT *will do.*)

PEASANT (*loosens the traces*). Bless me, Oh Lord! (*Takes the horse aside, turns it loose and walks over to his coat.*) I'm starvin'! The wife cut off a big chunk, and watch me eat it all. (*Comes up to the coat.*) Gone! I must've covered it with my coat. (*Lifts the coat.*) Not here either. That's really somethin'! (*Shakes the coat.*)

DEMON (*behind the bush*). Go on and look, look. It's here, right here! (*Sits down on it.*)

PEASANT (*raises the plow, shakes his coat again*). Strange, really strange! Nobody was here but the chunk's gone. If the birds got to it, there'd be crumbs. But there ain't a single crumb. Nobody was here but somebody took it.

DEMON (*rises and looks*). Now he'll bring me up.

PEASANT. Well, that's how it is. I won't die of hunger. Took is took. Let 'im eat hearty!

DEMON (*spits*). Oh, that damn peasant! He should be cursin' but he says: "Eat hearty!" Yuh can't do a thing with 'im. (*The* PEASANT *lies down, crosses himself, yawns, and falls asleep.*)

DEMON (*comes out from behind the bush*). Well Chief, what d'ya make of that! The Chief keeps on sayin': "You don't bring enough peasants to me in hell. Just look how many merchants, noblemen, and priests come in every day, but few peasants." How d'ya rein him in? There's no way to get at him. What more could I've done—I swiped his last chunk of bread. And he still didn't curse. I just don't know what to do now! I'll go and report. (*Disappears from sight.*)

ACT II

Hell. The CHIEF DEVIL *sits above all. The* DEVILS' CLERK *sits below at a table with writing materials.* GUARDS *stand at each side. To the right are five* DEMONS *of various types; to the left by the doors is the* DOORKEEPER; *the* DUDES' DEMON *stands in front of the* CHIEF.

DUDES' DEMON. My whole catch for three years is 263,753 people. They're all at my mercy now.

CHIEF. Fine. Thanks. Move on! (*The* DUDES' DEMON *goes off to the right.*)

CHIEF (*to the* CLERK). I'm tired. Is there much more business left? Whose reports have we got and whose are still missing?

CLERK (*counts on his fingers and points to the* DEMONS *standing to the right as he counts; when he names a* DEMON, *that one bows*). Report received from the Noblemen's Demon. In all he's snared 1,836. Received from the Merchants' Demon, 9,643. Received from the Priests', 1,517. Received from the Monks', 112. Received from the Judges', 3,423. Also just received from the Women's: 186,315 women, 17,438 girls. In all, 263,753.[1] Only two are left: the Lawyers' Demon and the Peasants'.

CHIEF. Well, it looks like we'll finish today. (*To the* DOORKEEPER.) Let the first one in. (*Enter the* LAWYERS' DEMON, *bows to the* CHIEF.)

CHIEF. Well now, how are things with you?

LAWYERS' DEMON (*laughing away and rubbing his hands*). Things are right as soot is white. I don't remember such a catch since the world began.

CHIEF. So, did you snare many?

LAWYERS' DEMON. It's not a matter of numbers. In number there aren't many, 1,350 men in all, but they're great guys. Such guys could take the place of devils. All by themselves they lead people astray worse than devils do. I started a new scam for them.

CHIEF. What's this new scam like?

LAWYERS' DEMON. It's like this: Lawyers before were in with the judges in cheating people. But now I've taught them to go it alone without the judges. Whoever pays the most, that's whose case they take. And they do so well, that they start cases where there are none. They're so good at it, that they cause people much more trouble than devils do.

CHIEF. I'll take a look, move on! (*The* LAWYERS' DEMON *goes off to the right.*)

CHIEF (*to the* DOORKEEPER). Let the last one in. (*Enter* PEASANTS' DEMON *with the chunk of bread, falls to his feet.*)

PEASANTS' DEMON. I can't go on any longer. Give me another job.

CHIEF. What other job? What's this nonsense? Get up, talk sense. Make your report, did you snare many peasants this week?

PEASANTS' DEMON (*crying*). Not a one!

CHIEF. What? Not a one! What do you mean not a one? What were you doing? Where have you been goofing off?

PEASANTS' DEMON (*sobbing*). I haven't been goofin' off. I've been knockin' myself out all the time, but I couldn't do anything. Look, I swiped the last chunk of bread from right under the nose of one of them, and he didn't curse but told me to eat hearty.

CHIEF. What?... What...are you muttering about? Blow your nose and talk sense, otherwise I can't make a thing out of what you're saying.

PEASANTS' DEMON. Well, a peasant was plowin', and I knew he only had a chunk of bread with him, and nothin' more to eat. I swiped the chunk from him. He should've cursed, but what does he do? He says: "Let the one who took it eat hearty." Here, I brought the chunk. Here it is.

CHIEF. Well, and what about the others?

PEASANTS' DEMON. But they're all alike—I didn't snare a single one.

CHIEF. How dare you come to me with empty hands? And what's more you bring some stinking chunk of bread! Are you trying to make fun of me? Huh? Do you want to be fed in hell for nothing? The others try hard, they work at it. Here, you see (*points to the* DEMONS), one got ten thousand, one, twenty thousand, one there got two hundred thousand. Even from the monks one nabbed a hundred and twelve. And you come with empty hands, and what's more you bring some chunk of bread and tell me tales! You're goofing off, not working. That's why they got away from you. Just wait, my friend, I'll teach you.

PEASANTS' DEMON. Don't have me punished, let me have my say! Those Demons have it easy with either noblemen or merchants, or women. It's a piece of cake. Show a nobleman a sable hat or an estate, and he's yurs right now to take wherever. It's the same with a merchant. Show 'im some money and stir up jealousy—and yuh've got 'im on a string and he won't get off. And it's also a piece of cake with women. Dresses and sweets—and do with them as yuh please. But just try foolin' with peasants. When he's at work from mornin' till night, and even well into the night, and won't begin a thing without God, how d'ya get to 'im? Master, release me from the peasants. I've knocked myself out with them, and I've also angered you.

CHIEF. Bull, deadbeat. There's no point to looking at others. They get the merchants, the noblemen, and the women because they know how to handle them, they keep on coming up with new twists. The Lawyers' got a completely new gimmick. Come up with something, too. Bragging about swiping a chunk of bread: what a coup! Cast a wide net and they'll get caught. But your goofing off gave them a way out—those peasants of yours have gotten the upper hand. Now they don't even care about their bread. If they get into that habit and teach their women, they'll get away altogether. Come up with something. Apply yourself as best you can.

PEASANTS' DEMON. I don't know what to come up with. Replace me. I can't anymore.

CHIEF (*angrily*). You can't! What, do you expect me to do the work for you?

PEASANTS' DEMON. I can't.

CHIEF. You can't? Just you wait. Hey! Get some rods over here. Whip him! (*The* GUARDS *seize the* DEMON *and flog him.*)

PEASANTS' DEMON. Oh! Oh! Oh!

CHIEF. Have you come up with something?

PEASANTS' DEMON. Oh! Oh! No, I can't.

CHIEF. Whip him some more. (*They flog him.*) Have you?

PEASANTS' DEMON. I have, yes, I have!

CHIEF. Well, out with it, what did you come up with?

PEASANTS' DEMON. I've come up with such a ruse that I'll have 'em all in my hands. Just let me hire on with the peasant as a farmhand; but I can't tell yuh about it now.

CHIEF. All right, just remember: If in three years you don't earn your bread, I'll rinse you in holy water.

PEASANTS' DEMON. They'll all be mine in three years.

CHIEF. Good. In three years I'll come and see for myself.

ACT III

A granary. Carts with grain wait.

SCENE 1

FARMHAND DEMON. *The* FARMHAND *is filling bushels from the wagon and the* PEASANT *is carrying them away.*

FARMHAND. Seven.

PEASANT. How many quarters?

FARMHAND (*looks at the marks on the door*). Exactly twenty-six quarters and this is the seventh bushel of the twenty-seventh.

PEASANT. It won't all go in, it's already full.

FARMHAND. Spread it around good.

PEASANT. Good idea. (*Carries away a bushel.*)

SCENE 2

FARMHAND (*alone, takes off his cap, exposing his horns*). He won't be back so quick now. I can straighten out my horns a bit. (*Horns are straightened.*) And I can take off my boots. Can't do it when he's around. (*Pulls off his boots exposing his hoofs. Sits down on the threshold.*) It's over two years already. Things are comin' to a head. We've got nowhere to put the grain. The only thing left is to teach 'im the last lesson. And then let the Chief come and see for himself. They'll be somethin' to show. He'll pay for that chunk of bread. (*A NEIGHBOR approaches.*)

SCENE 3

The FARMHAND hides his horns.[3]

NEIGHBOR. Howdy!

FARMHAND. Howdy!

NEIGHBOR. Where's the boss?

FARMHAND. Gone to spread the grain in the bin, it don't all go in.

NEIGHBOR. What luck your boss's havin'. No place to even store it. We're all amazed at all the grain yur boss produced these past two years. It's as if someone tipped 'im off. Last year it was dry—he planted the marsh. Us others lost everythin', but yur threshin' floor was chock full. This year was wet—he was smart enough to plant the hills. Everybody's was ruined, but yuh've got a bumper crop. And what grain, what grain! (*Shakes it in his hand and bites into it.*)

SCENE 4

PEASANT (*returns with an empty bushel*). Howdy, neighbor.

NEIGHBOR. Howdy. I'm just chewin' the fat with yur hand here, how yuh came up with where yuh planted. Everybody's jealous of yuh. The grain, all the grain yuh've got. Yuh couldn't eat it up in ten years.

PEASANT. That's thanks to Potap. (*Points to the* FARMHAND.) His luck. Last year I sent 'im to plow, and off he goes and plows up the marsh. I cursed 'im. But he talked me into plantin' there. That's what we did and it worked out for the best. And this year he hit it again, planted the hills.

NEIGHBOR. It's as if he knows what kind of year it'll be. Yeah, yuh've really got the grain. (*Silence.*) Anyway, I've come to ask for a sack of rye. I'm all out. I'll give it back next year.

PEASANT. All right, take it.

FARMHAND (*nudging the* PEASANT). Don't do it.

PEASANT. Enough talk, just take it.

NEIGHBOR. Thanks, I'll fetch a sack.

FARMHAND (*aside*). He still sticks to his old ways—just keeps on givin'. He don't listen to everything I say. Well, wait awhile—he'll soon stop givin'. (*Exit* NEIGHBOR.)

SCENE 5

PEASANT (*sits down on the threshold*). Why not give to a good man?

FARMHAND. To give is one thing, to get back's another. Lending's a downhill slide, but collectin'—an uphill pull. That's what the old-timers say.

PEASANT. No sweat, there's lots of grain.

FARMHAND. So what that there's lots?

PEASANT. There's not only enough till the next harvest but for two more years. What's there to do with it?

FARMHAND. What to do with it? From this grain here I'll make such good stuff for yuh that yuh'll be happy the rest of yur life.

PEASANT. What'll yuh make?

FARMHAND. A drink, that's what. Such a drink that if yuh're tired, it'll pick yuh up; if yuh're hungry, it'll fill yuh; if yuh're restless, it'll put yuh to sleep; if yuh're sad, it'll make yuh happy. If yuh're afraid, it'll give yuh courage. That's the kind of drink I'll make.

PEASANT. Bullshit!

FARMHAND. Again bullshit! Just like yuh didn't believe me when I first told yuh to plant grain in the marsh and then on the hills. Now yuh know. And yuh'll get to know about the drink the same way.

PEASANT. And what are yuh gonna to make it from?

FARMHAND. From this grain right here.

PEASANT. But won't that be a sin?

FARMHAND. Look at that! What's the sin here? Everything's given to man for happiness.

PEASANT. And where did'ya get so much smarts from, Potap? I see yuh as kind of a simple guy, a workin' stiff. Yuh've been here now for two years, never even took yur boots off once. And yuh know it all. How did'ya come by all this?

FARMHAND. I've been around.

PEASANT. So that drink there'll be a pick-up, eh?

FARMHAND. Yuh'll see—it's all to the good.

PEASANT. Well how do we go about makin' it?

FARMHAND. It's easy to make when yuh know how. Just need a boiler and a couple of pots.

PEASANT. And does it taste good?

FARMHAND. Sweet as honey. Once yuh've tasted it, yuh'll never give it up.

PEASANT. I'll go over to my neighbor, he had a boiler. Got to give it a try.

ACT IV

The set depicts a shed. In the center there is a sealed boiler over a fire with a pot and a spigot. The PEASANT *and the* FARMHAND.

SCENE 1

FARMHAND (*holds a glass under the spigot and drinks the booze*). Well, boss, it's ready.

PEASANT (*squats and watches*). That's really somethin'! Water comin' out of the mash. Why are yuh lettin' the water off first?

FARMHAND. That's not water, it's the real thing.

PEASANT. Why's it so light? I thought it'd be dark like beer. But it's just like water.

FARMHAND. Just you take a sniff of how it smells.

PEASANT (*sniffs*). Oh, smells good! Well now, well now, what's it like in yur mouth, let's have a taste. (*Tries to tear the glass from his hand.*)

FARMHAND. Hold on, you'll spill it. (*Turns off the spigot, drinks, and smacks his lips.*) Done! Here, drink.

PEASANT (*at first drinks a little, then more and more, empties the glass and gives it back*). How about some more. Yuh can't get the taste from a sip.

FARMHAND (*laughs*). So yuh liked it? (*Draws some more.*)

PEASANT (*drinks*). Well, that's somethin'! Have to call the wife. Hey, Marya, come over here. It's ready. Come on, move!

SCENE 2

The WIFE, *a* LITTLE GIRL, *and* THE FORMER.

WIFE. Well, what is it? Why are yuh yellin'?

PEASANT. Just you taste what we've cooked up. (*Hands her the glass.*) Take a sniff.

WIFE (*sniffs*). Wow!

PEASANT. Drink!

WIFE. Won't somethin' bad happen from it?

PEASANT. Drink, yuh fool!

WIFE (*drinks*). It's good!

PEASANT (*a little tipsy*). So yuh see it's good. Just wait and see what's comin'. Potap was sayin' it'll take the weariness out of yur bones. The young'll get old... I mean the old'll get young. Here I've just had two glasses and my whole body's straightened out. (*Showing off.*) See? Just wait, when we start drinkin' it every day, we'll become young again you and me. Well, Marya honey! (*Hugs her.*)

WIFE. Get lost! Look, it's made yuh nuts.

PEASANT. Ah, so yuh see! Yuh said me and Potap were wastin' grain, but what stuff we concocted. Huh? Speak up, good, ain't it?

WIFE. Why shouldn't it be good if it makes the old folks young. Look at how cheerful yuh are! And I'm also cheered up. Come on, join in! E...e...e... (*Sings.*)

PEASANT. That's it. We'll all be young, all cheerful.

WIFE. Got to call the mother-in-law, she's always cussin' and weary. She also needs changin'. She'll get younger and be nicer.

PEASANT (*drunk*). Call Mother, call her over. Hey, you, Mashka! Run and get Granny, and tell Gramps to come too. Say I want 'im to get down from the oven, that he's just lyin' around! We'll make 'im young. Well, quickly! One foot after the other, and off you go! (*The* LITTLE GIRL *runs off.*)

PEASANT (*to his* WIFE). How about another glass apiece! (*The* FARMHAND *fills and brings the glasses.*)

PEASANT (*drinks*). First it made us young up on top, in the tongue, then it went down into the hands. Now it's reached the feet. I feel my feet gettin' younger. Look, they're goin' by themselves. (*Begins to dance.*)

WIFE (*drinks*). Well now, Potap, yuh're a clever fellow, play a tune! (POTAP *takes a balalaika and plays. The* PEASANT *and his* WIFE *dance.*)

FARMHAND (*plays at the front of the stage, laughs and winks at them; he stops playing but they keep on dancing*). Yuh'll pay for that chunk of bread; these guys have had it now. They won't get away. Let 'im come and see.

SCENE 3

Enter a spry OLD WOMAN *and a very* OLD, WHITE-HAIRED MAN.

OLD MAN. What's goin' on, have yuh gone crazy? Everyone's workin' and here they're dancin'.

WIFE (*dances and claps her hands*). Up, up, up! (*Sings.*) I'm a sinner that's for sure. Only God alone is pure!

OLD WOMAN. Oh, yuh louse! The oven's not cleaned up and here she's dancin'!

PEASANT. Hold on, Momma. Look what we've got happenin' here! We're turnin' old folks into young uns. Here yuh go! Just drink! (*Hands her a glass.*)

OLD WOMAN. There's lots of water in the well. (*Sniffs.*) What the heck did'ya put in there? Whew, what a smell!

PEASANT AND WIFE. Go on and drink!

OLD WOMAN (*tastes it*). Wow! Can't yuh die from it?

WIFE. It'll make yuh more alive. Yuh'll be young again.

OLD WOMAN. Stop it! (*Drinks.*) It's really good! Better than beer. Well now, Papa, yuh have a taste too. (*The* GRANDFATHER *sits down and shakes his head.*)

FARMHAND. Leave him be. Now Granny here needs another glass. (*Offers it to the* GRANDMOTHER.)

OLD WOMAN. So long as nothin' comes of it? Oh, it burns! But nice.

WIFE. Drink up. Yuh'll feel it runnin' through yur veins.

OLD WOMAN. Well, probably should give it a try. (*Drinks.*)

WIFE. Has it gotten to yur feet yet?

OLD WOMAN. Yeah, it's gettin' there. Here it is, right here. It makes yuh feel so light. How about some more! (*Drinks more.*) Great! I'm young all over again.

PEASANT. I told yuh.

OLD WOMAN. Ah, too bad my old man ain't around! He'd see once more how I was as a young girl. (*The* FARMHAND *plays. The* PEASANT *and his* WIFE *dance.*)

OLD WOMAN (*goes to the middle*). Yuh call that dancin'? Here, I'll show yuh. (*Dances.*) That's how. Then like this and like that. Yuh see? (*The* GRAND-FATHER *goes up to the boiler and empties the booze on the ground.*)

PEASANT (*notices this and rushes to* GRANDFATHER). What have yuh done, yuh jerk? Lettin' out such good stuff! Oh, yuh old fart! (*Pushes him and holds his glass under the spigot.*) Yuh've let it all out.

GRANDFATHER. It's evil, not good. God made grain for yuh to feed yuhself and others, but yuh've turned it into a devil's drink. No good'll come of it. Drop this business, or else yuh'll perish and ruin the others! Yuh think it's a drink? It's fire, it'll burn yuh. (*Takes a piece of kindling from under the boiler and sets fire to it. The spilled booze burns. All look on in horror.*)

ACT V

The PEASANT'*s cottage. The* FARMHAND, *alone, with horns and hoofs showing.*

FARMHAND. Lots of grain, nowhere to put it, and he's got a real taste for it. We've been makin' booze again, and filled a barrel and hid it from the others. We won't let others drink for nothin'. We'll give drinks to the ones we need. Now today I told 'im to invite the old spongers and give 'em drinks so that they'd split 'im from his grandfather, and give nothin' to the grandfather. My time's up now, three years have passed and my work's done. Let the Chief come and see for himself. I'm not ashamed to show it even to 'im.

S C E N E 2

The CHIEF *appears out of the ground.*

CHIEF. Well, time's up! Have you earned your bread? I told you I'd come to see for myself. Have you gotten a rein on the peasant?

FARMHAND. Competely reined in. Judge for yourself. They'll get together here right away. Sit in the oven and watch what they'll do. Yuh'll be satisfied.

CHIEF (*climbs into the oven*). We'll see.

SCENE 3

Enter the PEASANT *and four* OLD MEN; *the* WIFE *follows. They sit down at the table. The* WIFE *sets the table and puts meat jelly and pies on it. The* OLD MEN *exchange greetings with the* FARMHAND.

FIRST OLD MAN. So, have yuh made much more of the drink?

FARMHAND. Yeah, we've made as much as we need.

SECOND OLD MAN. Come out all right?

FARMHAND. Better than the other batch.

SECOND OLD MAN. Where did'ya learn how?

FARMHAND. When yuh get around, yuh learn a lot.

THIRD OLD MAN. Yeah, yeah, yuh're a slick one.

PEASANT. Have some! (*The* WIFE *brings the booze and glasses.*)

WIFE (*takes the decanter and fills the glasses*). Welcome!

FIRST OLD MAN (*drinks*). To yur health! Ah, that's good! It goes right through yur joints! Now that's a drink! (*The other three* OLD MEN *do the same, one after the other. The* CHIEF *climbs out from an opening in the oven, the* FARMHAND *stands next to him.*)

FARMHAND (*to the* CHIEF). Watch what'll happen now. I'll trip his wife and she'll spill the glass. Before he didn't care care about the bread— just watch now what'll happen on account of a glass of booze.

PEASANT. Well now, Wife, pour some more and pass it around: to the old-timer here and then to Uncle Mikhaila.

WIFE (*fills the glasses and walks around the table; the* FARMHAND *trips her, she stumbles and spills the glass*). Oh, goodness gracious, I spilt it! What demon brought yuh here!

PEASANT (*to his* WIFE). What a clumsy bitch! Yuh're all thumbs and yuh talk 'bout others. Look at the good stuff yur spillin' on the floor!

WIFE. It wasn't on purpose, yuh know.

PEASANT. Beans, not on purpose. Wait till I get up, I'll teach yuh to spill booze on the ground. (*To the* FARMHAND.) And you too, yuh damn idiot, what are yuh fidgetin' for by the table? Go to hell! (*The* WIFE *fills the glasses again and serves the booze.*)

FARMHAND (*goes up to the oven and speaks to the* CHIEF). Yuh see: Before, he didn't care about his last piece of bread, but now for a glass of booze he nearly slugged his wife and sent me to you, the devil.

CHIEF. Good, very good. Congrats!

FARMHAND. Wait just a bit. Let 'em finish the whole bottle—watch what else'll happen. They're already talkin' smooth, sleek words, right away they'll begin butterin' each other up, and they'll all be as sly as foxes.

PEASANT. Well now, old-timers, what d'ya think of my business? My grandfather's been livin' with me, I've been feedin' 'im and feedin' 'im, and he's gone off to the uncle and wants to take his share of the place—to give away to the uncle. Decide what's right. Yuh're smart. Without yuh we're all lost. There's no one in the whole village compared to yuh. For instance, you, Ivan Fedotych, don't everyone say yuh're the number one man? As for me, Ivan Fedotych, I'll tell yuh the truth: I like yuh more than my own father and mother. And you, Mikhaila Stepanych, yuh're an old pal.

FIRST OLD MAN (*to the* PEASANT). It's good to talk with a good man— yuh'll get smart. That's so with you. Yuh can't find a soul to compare to yuh.

SECOND OLD MAN. Cuz yuh're smart and kind; that's why I like yuh.

THIRD OLD MAN. I can't tell yuh how I feel for yuh. I was tellin' the wife today.

FOURTH OLD MAN. Yuh're a pal, a real pal.

FARMHAND (*nudges the* CHIEF). Yuh see! It's all a lot of bullshit. When they're apart they bad-mouth each other. But see how they're layin' it on now, like foxes waggin' their tails. And it's all from drink.

CHIEF. The drink's good! Very good. If they keep on throwing the bull, they'll all be ours. Good, congrats.

FARMHAND. Wait a bit, let 'em finish another bottle, there'll be more yet.

WIFE (*serves them*). Here's another for yur health.

FIRST OLD MAN. Won't it be too much? Yur health! It's nice to drink with a good man.

SECOND OLD MAN. Got to have another. To the health of the host and hostess!

THIRD OLD MAN. Hey pals, here's to yuh!

FOURTH OLD MAN. What heady stuff! Let it roll! We'll fix everythin', cuz it's all up to me.

FIRST OLD MAN. To you—not to you, but to what those older than you'll say.

FOURTH OLD MAN. Older but dumber. Go kiss a cow's ass.

SECOND OLD MAN. Why're yuh cussin'? Eh, yuh damn fool!

THIRD OLD MAN. He's right. Cuz the host ain't treatin' us for nothin. He's got business. The business can be settled. You just treat. Show respect. Cuz you need me and I don't need you. Who're yuh? Yuh're brother to a pig.

PEASANT. That's what you are. What are yuh hollerin' for? Don't yuh know what's what? Yuh're all good at stuffin' yur faces.

FIRST OLD MAN. What are yuh, a smart ass? Come on, I'll knock yur nose off.

PEASANT. Who will?

SECOND OLD MAN. What a whiz! You go to hell! I don't wanna talk to yuh, I'm leavin'.

PEASANT (*holds him back*). What, d'ya wanna break up the party?

SECOND OLD MAN. Let go! I'll rap yuh one!

PEASANT. I won't! What right d'ya have?

SECOND OLD MAN. This one! (*Punches him.*)

PEASANT (*to the other* OLD MEN). Help! (*A brawl. The* PEASANT *and* OLD MEN *all speak at once.*)

FIRST OLD MAN. Cuz, yuh know, we're on a ro....ll!

SECOND OLD MAN. I can do it all!

THIRD OLD MAN. Bring some more!

PEASANT (*shouts to his* WIFE). Bring another bottle! (*They all sit down at the table again and drink.*)

FARMHAND (*to the* CHIEF). Did'ya see now? Their wolf's blood was talkin'. They've all become vicious like wolves.

CHIEF. It's a good drink! Congrats!

FARMHAND. Wait a bit. Let 'em finish a third bottle, there'll be more yet.

ACT VI

The set depicts a street. To the right OLD MEN *are sitting on logs with the* GRANDFATHER *between them. In the center* WOMEN, GIRLS, *and* BOYS *are in rings. Dance music is playing and they dance. Noise and drunken screams are heard from the cottage. An* OLD MAN *comes out and shouts in a drunken voice, followed by the* PEASANT *who takes him back.*

SCENE 1

GRANDFATHER. Oh, what sins, what sins! What more d'ya need? Work all week, a holiday comes, wash up, fix the harness, relax, sit a spell with the family, go out on the street to the old-timers, have a talk about community business. If yuh're young, what the heck, go on and have a good time! Over there they're havin' a real good time, it's fun to watch. It's decent, it's good. (*Screams in the cottage.*) But what's all that? They only upset folks and cheer up the devils. And it's all from fat livin'!

SCENE 2

Drunken MEN *come tumbling out of the cottage, go to the rings, shout, and grab the* GIRLS.

GIRLS. Let go, Uncle Karp, what's with yuh!
BOYS. We have to go to the lane. There's no havin' fun here! (*All exit except the drunken* MEN *and the* GRANDFATHER.)
PEASANT (*goes up to the* GRANDFATHER *and gives him the finger*). Well, what have yuh got? The old-timers promised to give it all to me. This is what yuh're gettin'! Here, chew on it! They gave everythin' to me, nothin' to you. They'll tell yuh so. (*The* FIRST, SECOND, THIRD, *and* FOURTH OLD MAN *all speak at once.*)
FIRST OLD MAN. Cuz I know what's what.
SECOND OLD MAN. I can get the best of any man, cuz I am what I am!
THIRD OLD MAN. Pal, pal o'mine, palsy-walsy!

FOURTH OLD MAN. Git on hearth, git on home, the missus got no place to roam! We're on a roll! (*The* OLD MEN *in pairs take hold of each other, walk off staggering, and exit—one pair, then the other. The* PEASANT *walks toward the house, stumbles before he gets there, falls down, and mumbles something unintelligible, like grunts. The* GRANDFATHER *gets up along with the* PEASANTS *and exits.*)

SCENE 3

Enter the CHIEF *and the* FARMHAND.

FARMHAND. Did'ya see? Now their pig's blood is talkin'. They've turned from wolves into pigs. (*Points to the* PEASANT.) There he is, like a boar in muck, gruntin'.

CHIEF. You've done it! First like foxes, then like wolves, and now they're like pigs. Well, that's some drink! But tell me, how did you make such a drink? You must have put some fox's, wolf's, and pig's blood into it.

FARMHAND. Nope, I only grew some extra grain. When he only had as much grain as he needed, he didn't care about a chunk of bread; but when he had room for no more, his fox's, wolf's, and pig's blood was roused. He always had beast's blood in him, only it had nowhere to go.

CHIEF. Good boy! You've earned your bread. Now if only they'd keep on drinking booze, we'll always have them in our hands.

Notes

INTRODUCTION

1. Leonard Schapiro, *Turgenev. His Life and Times* (Cambridge, Mass., 1978), 112.

2. Quoted in L. N. Tolstoy, *Polnoe sobranie sochinenii*, vol. 7 (Moscow, 1936), 380.

3. See L. N. Tolstoy, *Polnoe sobranie sochinenii*, vol. 7 (Moscow, 1936), 384, and Schapiro, 113.

4. Richard Stites, *The Woman's Liberation Movement in Russia. Feminism, Nihilism, and Bolshevism. 1860–1930* (Princeton, N.J., 1978), 38.

5. See Charles Moser, *Anti-nihilism in the Russian Novel of the 1860s* (The Hague, 1964).

6. For a full account of the relationship of *Notes from Underground* to this polemic, see Joseph Frank, *Dostoevsky. The Stir of Liberation: 1860–1865* (Princeton, 1986), 310–47.

7. Quoted in Irina Paperno, *Chernyshevsky and the Age of Realism. A Study in the Semiotics of Behavior* (Stanford, 1988), 28.

8. Letter of 2 July 1856, as quoted in L. N. Tolstoy, *Polnoe sobranie sochinenii*, vol. 7 (Moscow, 1936), 390.

9. "Just as I was getting better, L. N. Tolstoy dragged me over and read me his new comedy: it's so horrible, that his reading practically curled my hair": in a letter to Nekrasov of 7 March 1864, as quoted in the commentaries to Tolstoy's play (L. N. Tolstoy, *Polnoe sobranie sochinenii*, vol. 7 [Moscow, 1936], 393).

10. Later, in his tract *What Is Art?*, Tolstoy would insist that great art is always universally comprehensible and that it always must express the central religious idea of its day.

11. *The Realm of Darkness* will appear in volume 2 of this complete edition of Tolstoy's plays.

1.   *The Meaning of Man*, a work by the German philosopher Johann Gottlieb Fichte (1762–1814).

2.   This insult is meant to convey a radical intellectual or nihilist.

3.   Financial documents obliging one to pay a certain sum of money at a fixed time.

4.   The question marks enclosed in square brackets were made by the editors of the ninety-volume edition of *L. N. Tolstoy Complete Works*.

5.   Inadvertently Tolstoy gave two scenes the same number.

6.   Anatoly is married in the first version of this play.

7.   This is an entirely new character, who does not appear in the first version of this play.

A PRACTICAL MAN

1.   Jakov Vilimovich Bryus (1670–1735) was of Scottish origin (original surname, Bruce). A man of many talents in both civilian and military matters, he was one of Peter the Great's closest associates.

2.   The reference is to the so-called Bruce calendar (Bryusov kalendar'), a calendar, questionably ascribed to J. V. Bryus (see note 1), that prognosticates the weather and events for a two-hundred-year period.

3.   A corruption of the French word *depense* (expense).

4.   This is the same person that appears in the dramatis personae as [Olinka] Versina.

5.   Ivan Ilich corrupts this word by making it a plural.

AN UNCLE'S BLESSING

1.   Lydia is thinking about the hero of one of George Sand's tales.

FREE LOVE

1.   The name of the hero in George Sand's tale, "Teverino."

2.   The suffix -idze is a common ending for a surname in Georgian.

The name Chivchivchidze (pronounced chiv-chiv-CHID-ze) sounds as ridiculous in Russian as it does in English.

3.   The Caucusus was the setting for numerous adventure stories about desperate tribesman.

AN INFECTED FAMILY

1.   The reference here is to the decree published on 3 March 1861 (old style, 19 February) that emancipated the serfs. Household serfs were freed without land or payments; the serfs who worked the land were also given their freedom and approximately half the land they had been working for themselves. However, they had to pay for this land by making redemption payments.

2.   The reference is to George Henry Lewes (1817–78), the English writer and positivist.

3.   A concocted surname that literally means "those who jab/hit in the teeth."

4.   "New people" means the young radicals, as in the subtitle from N. Chernyshevsky's novel *What Is to Be Done? From Stories about New People*.

5.   The "other" person is the student, Aleksey Pavlovich Tverdynskoy, who is mentioned in this scene in another variant of this play. In creating the present version, Tolstoy apparently overlooked the fact that he was not mentioned in the dialogue between Venerovsky and Bekleshov.

6.   The reference is to Vasily Andreyevich Zolotov (1804–82), a famous pedagogue and author of children's books, including *A Pictoral History of Russia*, *History of Peter the Great*, and *A Russian ABC*.

7.   The Phoenician goddess of love, especially sexual love.

8.   A radical magazine published by Aleksandr Herzen and Nikolay Ogaryov in London from 1855–59, and in the years 1861, 1862, and 1869. It printed many things that could not appear in Russia, where it was imported illegally, widely read, and very influential.

9.   The mention of a practical man brings to mind the earlier unfinished play, *A Practical Man*. Who the practical man is in the existing frag-

ment cannot be said with certainty; however Prince Anatoly Osipych as described by Ivan Ilich (I,1) reminds us of Bekleshov.

10. This is a literal translation of the Russian proverb that corresponds to the English saying "so near and yet so far."

11. Two old customs (superstitions) are reflected here: being "first" was thought to assure dominance while throwing money assured prosperity.

12. The reference is to the English historian Henry Thomas Buckle (1821–62), who is best known for his two-volume *History of Civilization*.

13. A term derived from the name of the hero of I. A. Goncharov's novel *Oblomov*, to denote sluggishness, inertness, and apathy.

14. One of the fathers depicted in I. S. Turgenev's novel, *Fathers and Children*.

15. This is a reference to the charters regulating the relations between the landowner and his liberated serfs.

16. The name of Achilles' charioteer in the *Iliad*.

17. The French writer Victor Hugo (1802–85).

18. The present text reads: "The concrete can listen to you." The verb "listen" is a mistaken transcription for the verb "to confuse" (cf. the script forms of the verbs *slushat'* and *sputat'*).

19. This line contradicts what we learned before. From Ivan Mikhailovich's statement to Nikolaev (III,1,1) we are led to believe that the dowry will be given to Venerovsky on the day of the wedding or the next day. However, we learn from Bekleshov's remark to Venerovsky's relative (III,2,1) that Venerovsky was cheated and got nothing. Now it appears that he did receive the dowry.

20. Tolstoy has apparently forgotten that he never had Ivan Mikhailovich actually turn the deed over to Venerovsky. See footnote 19.

THE NIHILIST

1. She is mispronouncing the word nihilist.

2. She is mispronouncing the word organism.

3. That is, the first letter for Simon (written in Latin script), the French equivalent of Semyon.

4. The reference here is to the monks of the so-called Solovstsky Monastery located near the White Sea.

1. Luke 6:24–25.
2. Cf. Luke 16:20–22.

THE FIRST MOONSHINER

1. What this figure refers to is unclear, since it is the same one given for the Dudes' Demon alone. The total of the rest is 220,284.

2. Tolstoy apparently forgot to make the Demon hide his hoofs as well.